TRAILBLAZER

TRAILBLAZER

THE POWER OF BUSINESS AS
THE GREATEST PLATFORM FOR CHANGE

MARC BENIOFF
AND MONICA LANGLEY

**SIMON &
SCHUSTER**

London · New York · Sydney · Toronto · New Delhi

A CBS COMPANY

First published in the United States by Currency, an imprint of
Random House, a division of Penguin Random House LLC, 2019
First published in Great Britain by Simon & Schuster UK Ltd, 2019
A CBS COMPANY

The right of Marc Benioff and Monica Langley to be identified
as the authors of this work has been asserted in accordance with the
Copyright, Designs and Patents Act, 1988.

3 5 7 9 10 8 6 4

Simon & Schuster UK Ltd
1st Floor
222 Gray's Inn Road
London WC1X 8HB

www.simonandschuster.co.uk
www.simonandschuster.com.au
www.simonandschuster.co.in

Simon & Schuster Australia, Sydney
Simon & Schuster India, New Delhi

The author and publishers have made all reasonable efforts to
contact copyright-holders for permission, and apologise for
any omissions or errors in the form of credits given.
Corrections may be made to future printings.

A CIP catalogue record for this book is available from the British Library.

Hardback ISBN: 978-1-4711-8180-1
Trade Paperback ISBN: 978-1-4711-8181-8
eBook ISBN: 978-1-4711-8182-5

Book design by Andrea Lau
Printed in the UK by CPI Group (UK) Ltd, Croydon, CR0 4YY

CONTENTS

PART II Business Is the Greatest Platform for Change

PROLOGUE

This book's genesis took place in the summer of 1996 on a beautiful, blue-sky morning in San Francisco. The view of the bay from the window of my apartment would have been breathtaking to behold, but I didn't care. I was lying in bed, lacking the will or the energy to get up.

I had the greatest job I could ever have imagined at Oracle, one of the fastest-growing software companies in the world. Fresh out of college with a shaggy mane of hair and wacky collection of Hawaiian shirts, I had somehow caught the attention of the company's visionary founder, Larry Ellison. Within four years, I had been promoted to vice president, the youngest person ever in that position. Soon I had the multi-million-dollar salary, stock, and perks to go with it.

Yet there I was on a workday morning, frozen in place under the covers in my apartment on Telegraph Hill. I did not feel happy or fulfilled.

I was supposedly living the American dream, but I was lost.

Later that day, I managed to drag myself to the office, where I found Larry and told him about the malaise that had sunk in. His proposed solution was easy and direct: "Why don't you take a sabbatical? Take three months off, go take a look around." He added, "And pull yourself back together."

To be honest, I didn't really know what the word "sabbatical" meant, but Larry was my mentor, and I trusted his advice. Later that day, I called my friend Arjun Gupta to tell him what I was going through. He had just quit his job to start a new company, and he suggested we travel to Nepal and India together. I thought the trip sounded like a good diversion. I had no idea it would change the course of my life.

I eventually found myself in the city of Trivandrum, in southern India, near the backwaters of the Arabian Sea. We'd made our way there for one reason. A few years earlier, I'd briefly met Amma (meaning "mother"), Mata Amritanandamayi, a remarkably warm and wise woman known as "the hugging saint," who had offered spiritual guidance and comfort to untold thousands of followers. Secretly, I hoped that her wisdom and well-known healing embrace would help me find myself again.

With a chorus of Hindu chants and clouds of incense wafting over us, Arjun and I told her about business goals and how, we suspected, they were in some way connected to the existential confusion we both felt. Then Amma looked at us with her compassion and intensity, and said, "In your quest to succeed and make money, don't forget to do something for others."

With these words, the idea for Salesforce began to take shape. I knew in my head that I wanted to build a company that harnessed innovative new technology, but in my heart, I also wanted it to be committed to giving back. On that day in Trivandrum, the seed was planted. Two years later I left the Oracle nest to do just that.

When we signed the Salesforce incorporation papers in 1999, we wanted to make sure the notion of giving back was deeply ingrained in the fabric of its company culture. Of course, I hoped Salesforce would prosper by traditional measures—but I was equally determined that it would have a positive impact on the world. So, from the outset, we decided to identify the values that would serve as our bedrock. At first, they were trust, customer success, and innovation; later, we added a fourth, equality. We also decided that no matter how big the company grew, we would always set aside 1 percent of our equity, product, and employee time for charitable causes, an initiative we call the 1-1-1 philanthropic model.

Salesforce, if you're not familiar with us, pioneered the use of cloud computing as a way to provide essential "Customer Relationship Management" or CRM software to organizations of all sizes. As one of the first companies of our kind to allow our customers to download our products online and store their data securely in the cloud, we created a new business model that made smarter, more intuitive technology tools for large and small businesses accessible through subscriptions rather than onerous long-term contracts.

A few short years ago, I believed the chief reason Salesforce's market valuation had risen from $1 billion to more than $120 billion since we went public in 2004 was that we had done a commendable job of running the business. But I now know the most powerful engine of our success hasn't been our software, our people, or our business model, but rather, the decision we made in 1999 to orient our culture around *values*.

This isn't just my opinion; there's a growing pile of evidence that markets reward businesses that do good and that companies that have a social mission tend to be more successful. In a competitive business such as tech, where luring top talent can be the difference between profit and loss, it's often something intangible—like a diverse, inclusive, values-driven culture—that determines where the best and brightest talent decide to work.

In the last few complicated, uncertain years, through a mix of confusion, exhaustion, and exhilaration, I've come to appreciate how our values truly define who we are as a company. They're not some decorative spire perched atop our headquarters office tower in

San Francisco. They're part of the concrete and steel rebar in the basement. Time and again, they are what has kept the whole structure from keeling over.

I wrote this book to share all that I've learned on my journey, taking Salesforce from a poorly funded startup operating next door to my old San Francisco apartment to one of the fastest-growing technology companies that also ranks high on annual lists of the most admired businesses and best places to work. But this book isn't only about my journey—or about Salesforce. It's about how to create a culture where doing well is synonymous with doing good in order to thrive in a world where a company is only as strong as the principles it adopts. I don't pretend to have all the answers, but my hope is that whatever business you're in, this book will inspire you to bring your values to work.

PART I

VALUES CREATE VALUE

A NEW DIRECTION

Packed into the giant auditorium, in every seat and lining the walls, was a veritable army of global influence: leading politicians, executives, bureaucrats, academics, journalists, and policy experts. On either side of me sat my four fellow panelists, an esteemed group of technology CEOs and thought leaders. Behind us, the title of the keynote panel that was about to commence flashed on the screen in giant, intimidating type. It wasn't a title, really—more like a loaded question: *In Technology We Trust?*

As we sipped water and smoothed the creases in our jackets, our moderator, the business journalist Andrew Ross Sorkin, kicked things off by declaring that the public's eroding confidence in the judgment of technology companies was "the most pivotal and important discussion that's taking place right now, really in industry anywhere."

He was right. In early 2018, the tech industry was experiencing an acute crisis of trust. Recent revelations of alarming privacy breaches at Facebook, and even possible Russian-backed voter manipulation in the 2016 presidential election, were not sitting well with a large portion of the American public. The burning question on many of the minds gathered here at the annual World Economic Forum in Davos, Switzerland, was a deceptively simple one: *What are we going to do about it?*

Technology is a field to which I have devoted my entire career. I've often marveled at how today's advances in computing have transformed the way we live and work. During the last decade, the start of a period often referred to as the Fourth Industrial Revolution, we saw extraordinary advancements in artificial intelligence, quantum computing, genetic engineering, robotics, and 5G connectivity. Massive tributaries of digital information are now flowing at a speed and scale unthinkable even a decade ago while AI and robotics are breaking down barriers between humans and machines. Everyone and everything on the planet is becoming connected, creating complex business challenges and disruptions nobody could have foreseen.

I've always believed that technology holds the potential to flatten the world in wonderful ways; to foster a more open, diverse, trusting, and inclusive society while creating once-unthinkable opportunities for billions of people. Just one year from the publication of this book, it's likely that more people on the planet will have mobile phones than have running water or electricity in their homes.

But it had also become clear that technology is no panacea and such outcomes were far from guaranteed. New pressures and dangers had emerged, and with them came moral conundrums that none of us had ever considered. The global inequality gap had caused an erosion of trust in institutions, while complex social and economic issues including privacy, ethics, education, the future of work, and the health of the planet had begun to insert themselves, often uncomfortably, into the corporate agenda. On that snowy morning in Davos, one simple truth had become abundantly clear: These issues could no longer be dismissed as the domain of nonprofits, activists, or philanthropists. Every business, old or new, was struggling to figure out how to operate in a world where customers were beginning to hold them to higher moral and ethical standards.

A new day was dawning, whether we were prepared for it or not.

Meanwhile, the message I'd been hearing from my own employees, customers, and other stakeholders at Salesforce was simple: The world was changing, and the essential nature of what a business is, and how it should operate, needed to evolve. These weren't temporary, or incremental, shifts, either. They were structural and permanent. And to meet these challenges of the future, the one essential element every company needed most was what Salesforce had adopted two decades earlier as its number one value: trust.

In the panel's opening minutes, Ruth Porat, CFO of Alphabet (parent company of Google) remarked that she believed the public hadn't lost trust in Google; after all, she pointed out, people kept returning to its platforms daily to perform trillions of searches. It was a line of argument I'd heard from my tech colleagues many times before.

When it was my turn to speak, I said, "Trust has to be

your highest value in your company. And if it's not, something bad is going to happen."

I could sense a ripple of discomfort in the room. After a short pause, I began by pointing out other moments in history when regulators had fallen asleep at the wheel. I mentioned tech in the same breath as credit-default swaps, sugar, cigarettes—harmful products that companies had been allowed to peddle to customers, unconstrained by regulations. Our industry had been given a regulatory pass for years, I continued. "When the CEOs won't take responsibility," I said, "then I think you have no choice but for the government to come in."

When I arrived home from Davos, my phone began ringing nonstop. Leaders in the technology industry kept calling, one after another, to inform me that I had betrayed them. Apparently, I had broken ranks, or crossed some sort of imaginary line. And they didn't like it. My wife, Lynne, jokingly started calling me "the regulator."

Crawling out on that limb was, at the time, a scary feeling. As a lifelong champion of technology, I felt deeply conflicted about my new role as its apparent chief critic. But no amount of scorn could persuade me that growth, innovation, profit, or any other motive, was more critical to the success of a business than building and sustaining people's trust.

I decided to write this book because I genuinely believe we are on the brink of a *Fifth* Industrial Revolution, one in which trust will be earned by those companies that apply the technologies developed in the Fourth to improving the state of the world. In the future, innovation cannot advance in a positive direction unless it's grounded in genuine and continued efforts to lift up all of humanity. Companies, and the people who lead them, can no longer afford to separate business objectives from the social issues surrounding them. They can no longer view their mission as a set of binary choices: growing vs. giving back, making a profit vs. promoting the public good, or innovating vs. making the world a better place.

Rather, it must be *and*. Doing well by doing good is no longer just a competitive advantage. It's becoming a business imperative.

I wrote this book because I believe that every company and every individual—from new hires to those sitting in the corner office—has the potential to become a platform for change. Not only because it's the right thing to do, but also because in the future, success will demand it.

On that snowy weekend in Davos in 2018, I finally realized that the tables had turned. Salesforce, the company I'd led for almost twenty years, was guiding me in a new direction.

Lots of businesses talk about values, but in turbulent times, when they matter most, executives often forget to operationalize them. They see values as expensive luxuries that should remain nailed harmlessly to the wall when making major business decisions. If some new product or initiative does not seem to advance the company's stated values, many CEOs seek solace by distancing themselves. They rationalize that it's really not their business to monitor how people use the products they offer to the world.

I've written about corporate responsibility in my three

previous books. In *Compassionate Capitalism* I first wrote about how corporations can make doing good an integral part of doing well; in *The Business of Changing the World* I shared the stories of fellow CEOs who made philanthropy a key part of their businesses. In *Behind the Cloud* I chronicled the first decade of both building the business of Salesforce and integrating philanthropy into the fabric of the company.

But now I've written *Trailblazer* with the realization of what was really happening at Salesforce. A series of leadership trials and challenges we faced—and the bumpy, sometimes painful, occasionally inspiring, process of addressing them—ultimately changed how I understood the future of business, upending my perception of what made the company work.

If there's one thing that the experiences I've shared in these pages taught me, it's that tough times are when values and culture matter most. And whether or not we got it right on the first try, the paths we've chosen at Salesforce have been the ones that best upheld our collective values. Not just sometimes, but always.

Had it been only the company's executive leadership guiding these decisions, the story would have unfolded differently. But we never would have weathered the challenges and reached the heights you'll read about in these pages had it not been for the fact that just about every important decision we've made was inspired, if not guided, by our stakeholders—our employees, customers, partners, investors, and the communities where we live and work.

To succeed in the future, every person in every business will need to forge new paths. Because no matter what you do or where you work, everyone can contribute to building a successful business *and* a better world. So if the central premise of this book can be boiled down to a single point, it's this: A culture rooted in values creates value.

My sincere hope is that this book will inspire you to look inside yourself, ask the right questions, and blaze your own trail. What you do next matters.

ONE

BEGINNINGS

The Benioffs of San Francisco

Here are two surprising personal tidbits about me: I graduated from college. Not only that, I majored in business.

Among my peers in the tech sector, those résumé points are something of a novelty. Countless Silicon Valley founders and CEOs proudly confess to quitting school to pursue their dreams. It's no secret why the story of the "dropout billionaire" is so predominant. It's the kind of compelling personal narrative that magazine editors and Hollywood screenwriters love. It also props up the old mythology that in America, a person's success is largely a matter of sheer determination and will. A genuine hero is someone who learns about business by building one.

I'm a big believer in the enlightening, civilizing powers of higher education, full stop. But I'm not convinced that attending college makes you a superior entrepreneur. The courses I took at the University of Southern California made me a more well-rounded and curious person, but the toughest business challenges I've faced, especially lately, are those that my professors in the 1980s simply couldn't have anticipated.

There's one way in which I do fit the profile of the archetypal tech entrepreneur, however. My first, most formative business classroom wasn't a classroom at all.

It wasn't my basement computer lab, or my first job, or the boardrooms where I made those early, tentative pitches to potential Salesforce investors. My classroom sat on four radial tires and ran on leaded gas. It was my father's 1970 Buick station wagon.

The Benioff family Buick was a whale of an automobile nearly 19 feet long with simulated wood paneling. Driving around with my dad on hot summer afternoons, my bare legs stuck to the vinyl seats. Most of the time our trusty wagon was just a means of getting my parents, my two sisters, and me from point A to point B. Sundays were different, though. On Sundays it became a delivery vehicle.

My father, Russell, owned a chain of dress shops called Stuart's Apparel. On weekends, he'd run a circuit around the San Francisco Bay Area transferring merchandise between his six locations, and he often brought me along to help. We'd park the Buick near the stockroom door, lower the tailgate, and march in and out with bolts of wool, linen, rayon, cotton, poplin, and polyester draped in our arms.

His shops were scattered all over the Bay Area, sometimes up to an hour's drive from San Francisco; so our Sunday ritual often consumed the better part of a day. When I wasn't staring out the window lost in my interior world, I passed the time thinking about how my father worked.

During the week, Dad would gather all the data on what items were selling and transfer the most popular merchandise to the best-performing stores. I'd overhear him say things like "We need pink angora sweaters at Valley Fair" and off he'd dash, leaving his half-eaten dinner behind. At one point in the 1970s, fox and rabbit coats took off, and for more evenings in a row than I could count, so did Dad. He'd get the call from one of his managers, hang his merchandise on a metal bar he'd installed in the Buick's cargo space, and roar off.

It's fair to say that my dad wasn't bursting with personality. He was a giant at six foot seven, not unlike myself, but a decidedly gentle one: affable, down-to-earth, impeccably polite, and always caring, but like many men of his generation, emotionally restrained. Having lived through the Great Depression, he was frugal throughout his life. He shopped for clothes mostly on sale racks at big-and-tall stores, and every car he bought—including the Buick—was used.

Dad's father, Fred Benioff, was one of three Benioff brothers who immigrated with their father to San Francisco from Kiev (then part of the Russian Empire) in the late nineteenth century to enter the fur trade. Beyond that, I know very little about Fred; he left his wife and kids when my dad was young and they never spoke again. Dad's mother, Helen, eventually managed to wrestle away control of the Benioff fur business from her ex-husband and ran it herself. The business had outlets all over the West, which forced her to work grueling hours, so my dad and his brother were raised with the help of family friends.

In 1966, the year I turned two, Dad decided to quit the family business to strike out on his own—and before long he was not only the CEO of Stuart's Apparel, but also the CFO, chief buyer, director of marketing, and head of sales. This meant that most nights, when he wasn't traveling to Los Angeles or New York—as he often did to scour their garment districts for new styles—he sat at the kitchen table until eleven o'clock, doing the books by hand. Because he managed the inventory for all six stores himself, his weekends were mostly consumed by shuttling dresses and sportswear from one location to another. His only indulgences were playing dominoes and occasionally going fishing or hunting.

I never liked the idea of killing anything, but I spent many days as a boy with a 12-gauge shotgun over my shoulder. Hunting ducks, doves, deer, and even wild pigs with my father in the orange groves of California's San Joaquin Valley, and fishing in the Truckee River near Lake Tahoe, were as much a part of my childhood as hauling around women's slacks and blouses. I didn't particularly enjoy these activities—or like them at all, really—but these were the activities I could do with my dad.

Those Sundays in the car shuttling merchandise from store to store were long and tedious. But they did help me realize early on that I was not a fan of the retail business, one of several glaring differences between my father and me. Russell Benioff was an outdoorsman and a wizard with tools and lumber, but he wasn't technically-minded. I, on the other hand, was so fascinated by electronic equipment that, according to my mother, Joelle, I took the family telephone apart and put it back together at the age of four. Every time my maternal grandmother visited, I begged her to take me to Radio Shack.

As far back as I can remember, I was the shy kid who rarely had play dates, avoided group activities, and preferred the company of my golden retriever, Brandy, to that of just about any human being. My dad wasn't the type to express concern over my social development, but my behavior worried my mother. She couldn't get me to play baseball or even come out to say hello to her friends when they visited. I wasn't particularly motivated by school, either: Once, when a kindergarten teacher asked me to draw a circle, I looked her straight in the eye and defiantly drew a line. Even though Mom left countless teacher meetings in tears, she continued to give me a long leash to pursue my passions, which certainly weren't in the classroom.

When I was twelve, I packed up my second-floor bedroom and moved down to the basement, where I could pursue my singular passion free of interruption. I bought my first computer, a TRS-80 from Radio Shack, two years later and immediately withdrew from the analog world. After learning the basics of coding at fifteen, I wrote a simple program called "How to Juggle." I sent it to a computer magazine and they paid me $75 for it. Suffice it to say that by that point, I was hooked.

On my sixteenth birthday, I traded my TRS-80 in for an Atari 800 with a freestanding disc drive and a printer. That summer, I started working part time at ComputerLand and in my off hours founded my first company, which I christened with an outrageously sexy name: Basic Computers, after the BASIC programming language with which I had fallen in love.

I began writing reviews of computer games; when I noticed some games had software bugs, I wrote to the developers and offered to fix them for free. Soon I started programming games of my own. My first creation, Quest for Power, had a convoluted plot involving King Arthur and Sir Galahad and required players to vanquish a series of foes in pursuit of the Scroll of Truth.

This game, and many more that I created, helped me earn more than $5,000 in six months, which was a fortune for someone my age. I used the money to buy my first car, a black Toyota Supra, and vanity plates that read MRB 82. The money I earned from those games over the years eventually paid for college.

Looking back, I continue to marvel at the fact that my parents not only tolerated my eccentric behavior, but gave me enough independence to fully indulge it. When I tell people about how I was allowed to turn our basement into my own private residence at age twelve, they are always (justifiably) astonished. In retrospect, I imagine my mother was less than thrilled when I announced, on the very day I got my driver's license, that I needed to make a business trip to a computer company in Mountain View, much farther than I had ever driven on my own. But she let me go. And that summer, when I asked if I could fly to England, alone, to research castles for my games, Mom gave me her blessing, so long as I stayed with friends of hers in Leeds and promised to call home every night.

My mother claims that she indulged me because she knew I was stubborn and wouldn't take no for an answer. The truth, I know, is that she saw something in me that others didn't and allowed me to pursue it, even if doing so made it nearly impossible for her to get a good night's sleep. Neither she nor my father fully understood what I found so fascinating about computers, but they respected my drive, my strong will, and my unwavering commitment to things I cared about, and sensed that these values would serve me well when I got older. They turned out to be right.

A Different Kind of Legacy

In the hospital after I was born, my mother was handed a form to assign a legal name to her one-day-old child. The name Marc had been previously decided in honor of my grandfather Marvin, but for my middle name, she wrote down her maiden name, Lewis. Shortly thereafter, in a rare fit of enthusiasm, my dad decided to scratch off Lewis and write his first name, Russell, in its place. My mother approved. "Well, gee," she thought, "that's wonderful that he is so excited to have a son!"

I'm not sure I ever became the son my father imagined that day. I'm thankful he lived long enough to see Salesforce blossom and I know he was proud of me. We'd always been very different people, and it was clear, very early on, that someday taking over his business was never in the cards for me. Yet there's no doubt that my father's career as a businessman had a profound influence on mine.

During those endless Sundays in the station wagon, I was struck by my father's work ethic and unwavering integrity. There was no funny business whatsoever with the financials or inventory. Everything was done strictly by the book. To him, all business decisions were black or white, right or wrong. As a father, he could be distant at times, but he built deep, genuine relationships at work and would do whatever it took to keep his employees and customers happy—as if *that* were the entire point of a business.

Even as a teenager, when I would think about how much time

my dad spent traveling to meet with suppliers, ferrying inventory around, and minding the company ledgers, I was astounded by how difficult it was to run a business in the analog age. To me, he seemed enslaved by the rudimentary tasks of commerce; he got so buried in the weeds that he rarely had time to focus on the big picture.

I know that my father didn't like to talk about computers and couldn't really comprehend their increasing power, but sometimes, as we unpacked merchandise, I would implore him to let me build him a customer database to streamline the tedious work of sending out promotional flyers. Eventually, he grudgingly agreed, but it's fair to say he never quite embraced the notion that software had the potential to make his day-to-day operations demonstrably easier and more efficient.

In 1999, when I told my father I was quitting my lucrative executive job at Oracle to found a company of my own, he warned against it. He told me I had a good thing going at Oracle, and he wasn't wrong; I was lucky enough to be earning a great salary, and I had a terrific boss in Larry Ellison. But I'd already made up my mind. Looking back, I can't help but wonder if he might have responded differently had he known that his experiences had been the kindling for the idea that was now smoldering inside me.

The big idea behind Salesforce was to make it easy for any business to access all of the software it needed to manage its operations and customer relationships from the cloud (which in those days was simply known as the Internet). Rather than having to buy an acre of costly servers, license software from Oracle or Microsoft, and hire an army of IT specialists to install it—and then upgrade to a new version every few years—I wanted small-business owners like Dad to be able to pay one flat subscription fee to access the latest software instantly in their Web browser with no more effort than it takes to buy a book on Amazon.

In business terms, Salesforce is engaged in customer relationship management, or CRM, but the service we provide is a lot broader, more essential, and more intimate than it sounds. Our software may be invisible to consumers, but inside a company, Salesforce is a vital piece of infrastructure. After all, the most valued asset of any company is its relationship with its customers, and our vision was to offer businesses of all sizes smarter, more intuitive ways to connect with those customers across sales, marketing, customer service, and e-commerce. Eventually, we began providing tools to help those companies create new processes, customize apps, analyze data, and create predictive models.

Though it seems obvious now, it took a while for me to link the evolution of this big idea back to its source: my father's struggles as the owner of Stuart's Apparel. If I hadn't seen, up close, the many hats he had to wear while running a small business, and how many countless hours were required just to keep the operation functioning, I wouldn't have understood what the kind of services Salesforce offers would mean to people just like him.

From a young age, I'd always thought of myself as my own man, distinct from my father in so many ways. But founding Salesforce was, to some extent, the act of a dutiful son. It's as if I was trying to reach back in time and lighten my father's burdens. I may not have followed in his footsteps by taking the helm of the company he owned, but in the end, his business problems were the ones I devoted my career to solving.

Even beyond that, I've come to see that in some sense, everything about Salesforce's business model, and my approach to leadership, reflects my father's guidance. His genuine concern for customers and employees clearly rubbed off on me: That explains why "customer success" is one of Salesforce's core values. He also drilled into me the importance of pristine accounting practices, which probably explains why trust and transparency have always been so important to me.

Without my mother's selfless love and faith in me, I'm not sure how I would have turned out. But it's also clear that my career is inextricably tied to the lessons I learned from my father, which is a testament to how powerful mentors can be. But he wasn't my only teacher.

When we founded Salesforce, I wasn't interested in building a viable little business. I wanted it to have global magnitude, and become the leader in its industry, while also serving the greater good.

This is a goal that was unquestionably inspired by another member of the Benioff clan.

A Passion for Progress

During my summer breaks, starting when I was about seven, the Benioffs' Buick started making cargo runs of another kind. These deliveries were made exclusively to my maternal grandfather, Marvin Lewis. The merchandise under transfer was me.

My grandfather ran a prominent legal practice out of the de Young Building, a venerable eleven-story temple of commerce at the north corner of Kearny and Market streets in downtown San Francisco. As a kid, I thought most tall buildings looked the same, but Grandpa made sure I understood that this one was special. Every time my parents dropped me off for a visit, he'd remind me that when the de Young Building first opened in the roaring 1890s, it was the tallest tower on the West Coast.

Within seconds of my arrival, my grandfather would grab his coat and hat and steer me out the door. Down the elevator we'd go, into the marbled lobby, through the stately brass doors, and onto the teeming sidewalk. Grandpa would set off at a brisk pace and I'd do my best to keep up, eager to play my part in these parades of two.

I call these walks parades because that's how they felt. With his regal thatch of silver hair and impeccably tailored suits, Marvin Lewis was larger than life. To the same degree that my father was modest and reserved, my mom's dad was a blustery showman. He felt most alive when all eyes were on him, and it's safe to say they usually were.

As an attorney, Grandpa made a name for himself by taking on spectacular, difficult cases. He pioneered the legal concept of psychic injury. In a 1959 case, he won a then-astounding sum of $101,000 for a woman who sued her landlord after falling through a wooden stairway at her apartment. The woman, June Daimare, sued her landlord for damages, and was awarded $101,000 by the judge. He was the founder and first president of the California Trial Lawyers Association and later became president of the American Trial Lawyers Association. Whether he was arguing a case or just taking an afternoon stroll with his shy, chubby, mop-haired grandson, everything he did felt like an event.

These journeys of ours had no set route or destination, but they absolutely served a purpose. They were educational tours for my benefit, loosely organized around Grandpa's favorite theme: *progress*.

Marvin Lewis had a passion for big, ambitious civic projects, which explains his reverence for the de Young Building. Once, when our path took us to the construction site for the Transamerica Pyramid, he turned to me and said: "Here's how the city will grow."

Another time, during a stop at Mission Bay—then a desolate area that was once home to shipyards, foundries, warehouses, and factories—he boldly (and correctly) proclaimed that one day, "this will be the future of San Francisco."

I was convinced he had the power to see the future.

Grandpa also dabbled in politics, and at the close of the Second World War he began an eleven-year stint as a San Francisco city supervisor. In that role, he focused his considerable powers of persuasion on one civic priority: building a new, thoroughly modern mass transit system.

In 1954, Marvin Lewis unveiled a plan for a space-age, fifteen-mile monorail that would run through the heart of downtown. The federal bond issue he led to finance this new entity, which came to be known as Bay Area Rapid Transit, was the largest local bond ever approved in the United States. BART finally opened in 1972 to much acclaim. It was, as described by *Fortune,* "the finest rapid transit line in the world." Its space-age automated cars were light, aerodynamic, and controlled entirely by computers.

My grandfather's futuristic vision for BART wasn't just about shiny fast trains. He didn't believe in building impressive things just for the sake of building impressive things. His vision was also guided by the way he defined *progress.* In his mind, no civic project really mattered unless it also furthered what he saw as San Francisco's bedrock values: opportunity, equality, and inclusion.

By enabling the city's residents to travel quickly and inexpensively between downtown and the suburbs, he knew BART would give them access to better jobs and more opportunities for life enrichment. He also knew it would reduce the growing congestion on the bridges spanning the Bay and mitigate the environmental problems this traffic caused.

My grandfather's commitment to opportunity for all wasn't an affectation. During our walking tours, we sometimes came across a homeless person on Market Street. He'd pull out his wallet and hand over a $20 bill, a considerable sum to give a stranger back then. To him, BART was an extension of the same altruism. He thought the city owed it to its citizens to invest in ambitious infrastructure projects, provided they served the common good.

My father's influence on Salesforce was foundational, but it was mostly quiet, pragmatic, and compassionate, much like the man himself. Grandpa's contribution, on the other hand, was loud, ambitious, spiritual, and altogether impossible to ignore.

On the day we signed the incorporation papers, I knew that the measure of my success as a CEO—and, in truth, as a person— would be the extent to which every future employee found meaning in his or her work. If my father's example had taught me anything, it was that meaning isn't about what kind of work you do or how much money you make. It's grounded in a mindset in which your work, and the integrity with which you perform it, really matters.

That's when I made it my top priority to create the kind of culture where people felt that what they did when they arrived at the office every day truly mattered, that they were consistently contributing to something other than just the company's bottom line with their efforts. By incorporating volunteerism and giving back at the start, we could build a culture with meaning.

So I decided that no matter how much Salesforce grew, it would donate 1 percent of its product, 1 percent of its equity, and 1 percent of its employees' time to help nonprofits and charities. There's no doubt in my mind that this decision was inspired, at least in part, by my grandfather's view that progress is supposed to lift people up.

We wrote down our first set of values upon the founding of Salesforce in the spring of 1999. Even as a tiny start-up, we had a grand vision to create a world-class Internet company and leader in sales force automation. Achieving this would demand more than simply hiring good people and shipping a functional product. Our success would rest upon our ability to build a culture that adhered to our values.

The great miscalculation of the age is the idea that businesses have to make a choice: to become profitable, or to become platforms for change. This is not the case. According to a 2018 Global Strategy Group study, 81 percent of Americans agree that "corporations should take action to address important issues facing society," and 76 percent agreed that corporations should "stand up for what they believe politically regardless of whether or not it is controversial." And these numbers have been rising steadily, and will continue to rise in lockstep with the complexity of the world in which we live.

Salesforce has done well by any measure, but it's also done good. As I write this, two decades later, our 1-1-1 corporate philanthropy program has already generated nearly $300 million in grants and

4 million hours of employee volunteer time. More than forty thousand nonprofits and nongovernmental entities (NGOs) use Salesforce's products for free or for a steep discount. I've always seen this as a tribute to my grandfather, and part of what makes our company different from most.

But it wasn't until a few years ago that the degree to which Salesforce truly is a distillation of my grandfather's legacy came into focus. More than anyone else I've ever known, he embodied a pioneer spirit. He had a vision for how a better world might look and the personal conviction to pursue it. Conceiving of BART, and putting together the financing to make that vision a reality, wasn't the work of a pragmatist. It was a triumph of imagination guided by values.

Imagination Guided by Values

I realize that the personal stories I've shared here might give you the wrong impression about this book. It's not intended to be a memoir, or some exercise in hagiography.

At the same time, companies are ultimately defined by people, and those people either choose to absorb the lessons of their teachers and mentors or actively work against them. As Salesforce's founder and co-CEO, I can't expect you to evaluate what I think about the future of business unless you understand where I'm coming from. The ideas I want to share in these pages won't stick if they sound like empty platitudes.

Maybe you saw some similarities between my upbringing and yours, or perhaps none whatsoever. In either case, that's okay. I think we can all agree that there are thousands of paths to the same destination. My hope is that you will find something useful in the lessons I absorbed from my earliest and most formative business mentors: my dad, who gave me an unvarnished look at the small, ceaseless operational challenges and pain points of small-business owners and showed me the value of honesty, trust, and putting employees and customers first, and my grandpa, who taught me to think about the world in expansive terms. From him I learned that you can't live your beliefs to the fullest unless you develop the imagination and the confidence to express them in bold, meaningful ways.

These weren't my only mentors, of course, and you'll read about others throughout the book. But it would be impossible to introduce the concept of mentorship without telling you about the strong women I've been fortunate to have in my family—and from whom I've learned different but important life lessons. My paternal grandmother, Helen Benioff, showed me the meaning of dogged determination; after her husband took all the family's money and left her with their two young sons, she seized control of the family fur business and became a successful woman proprietor, a rare feat at the time. My maternal grandmother, Frederica Lewis, made sure I learned the value of patience and hard work, as she drove me to odd jobs so I could earn enough money to buy my first computer at Radio Shack (and then wrote the music for my Atari games). My mother, Joelle Benioff, taught me that nothing is more valuable than a parent's love and encouragement when few others believe in you, and she is and always has been my biggest supporter.

My wife, Lynne, is my ultimate inspiration, my partner in all things, and the core of our family. When I come home, she often tells me: "Get down from your soapbox and let's talk about what's really important here." We discuss the urgency of what needs to be done, from helping to eradicate San Francisco's homeless crisis and getting families off the streets, to improving healthcare for children by building world-class hospitals in the Bay Area, to protecting the planet's oceans from pollution. It's impossible to overstate how much wisdom there is to be gleaned from the people closest to us about the things that truly matter.

Today, more than ever, we need to be seeking out as much wisdom as we can. The Fourth Industrial Revolution has advanced our knowledge and unleashed new transformative capabilities. It's also brought us to an urgent moment in history as we confront the challenges of increasing inequality and growing concern for our planet. The Fifth Industrial Revolution will demand a fundamental change to the nature of business, and our roles in it, to address the global challenges ahead and improve the state of our world.

Whether you manage thousands of employees, lead a small team, or have just draped an ID badge around your neck for the first time, it's important to stop thinking like a passenger along for the ride. You must set aside the fear of the unfamiliar, use your values as a compass, and start blazing a new trail.

It's time we all developed a passion for progress, and the imagination to realize it.

A better future depends on us.

TWO

VALUES

What You Do Matters

I was in a car crawling through the fog on Interstate 280 toward San Francisco when the call lit up my phone. I glanced at the screen to check the number.

I recognized the Indianapolis area code immediately.

I'd just spent a couple of hours giving a talk at the Computer History Museum in Mountain View and I'd been looking forward to having a little time on the road to decompress, maybe even let my mind wander a bit. Those plans were instantly abandoned. I knew I had to pick up.

The caller, Scott McCorkle, wasn't one to ring me at the end of a workday for a chat. As the head of Salesforce's Marketing Cloud division, Scott oversaw twelve hundred people in Indianapolis, our largest hub outside San Francisco.

Scott had been dealing with a disturbing situation, and I assumed that he needed my input. As soon as I answered, I could tell from the ominous tone in his voice that I'd assumed correctly.

"Look, Marc," he said, "you don't understand what's happening here."

On that foggy March day in 2015, my executive team and I had been monitoring events in Indiana, where the state legislature had passed a bill called the Religious Freedom Restoration Act. On its face, the bill would enable people of faith to resist unwelcome governmental infringements on their principles. In practice, however, we knew it was designed to give the state's business owners legal cover to discriminate against LGBTQ customers if their religious views compelled them to do so.

We'd sent a letter asking the governor to reject the bill. As one of the state's largest tech employers, we thought that our strong opposition, combined with similar protests from Indiana-based businesses such as Cummins, Eli Lilly, and Roche Diagnostics, would ensure it never became law. Even so, we'd sent word to our employees in Indiana that if they felt threatened, Salesforce would move them to another office. I felt great relief that Cindy Robbins, our Head of Employee Success (Human Resources) at the time, was already on the case.

Indiana was just one of several brushfires we'd been dealing with, and it hadn't been at the top of my mind. In a matter of seconds, that changed. Scott had called to deliver the worst possible news: Indiana governor Mike Pence had decided to sign the legislation.

"This is just not right," Scott said. "It's discrimination. Our employees are afraid."

I agreed with Scott completely and thanked him for calling to let me know. But he wasn't just reaching out to keep me updated. He'd called to pose a question that caught me completely off guard:

"What are *you* going to do about it?"

In 2015, I thought I was doing a fine job running Salesforce. After sixteen years of hard work, we were the clear global leader in CRM, with annual revenues approaching $10 billion. We'd become one of the world's top software providers and had recently expanded our product line. By every possible standard, Salesforce was a roaring success. Beyond that, I was proud of the positive, purposeful culture we'd built around our three founding values: trust, customer success, and innovation.

So I'll admit it. Riding up the highway, I thought I was standing on pretty firm moral ground. I'd grown so contented with the state of things that before Scott punched in my number, the thought of doubling down in Indiana hadn't crossed my mind.

I told Scott I would have to call him back.

All at once, the doubts poured in. I knew this law was terribly wrong. But I also knew that as a native San Franciscan, I took the notion of tolerance for granted and couldn't fully comprehend the forces behind this initiative. Beyond that, I wasn't sure how Salesforce, or any company, ought to handle an act of government that expressly discriminated against its LGBTQ employees. After all, I was the CEO of a tech company, not a politician. It's always been the government's job to keep businesses in check, not the other way around.

The employee emails and phone calls started trickling in from every corner of the company and soon picked up steam. Our people weren't just encouraging their CEO to do something bold to fight this law, they were demanding it. Just when I thought I had the world figured out, I found myself alone in unfamiliar territory.

I'd grown accustomed to taking on industry competitors like Oracle, Microsoft, and SAP, but fighting a state's legislature and governor was another story. I am a staunch believer in the democratic process, and in this case the voters, through their elected officials, had spoken.

At the same time, I knew there was something larger at stake. How we responded would say a lot about the kind of company Salesforce had become. Our employees in Indiana were telling me they feared living and working in a state that allowed discrimination and it was my job to protect and reassure them.

It might surprise some readers to learn that when it comes to politics, I was at one time a Republican, but now I'm an independent. I've given advice to both George W. Bush and Barack Obama.

I personally held a fundraiser for Hillary Clinton during the 2016 campaign, but I had no problem coming to the Trump White House in my capacity as a business leader to talk about workforce development and technology training programs. Salesforce is not a political organization and our values don't come with party affiliations.

As I stared out the car window, I could see the outlines of landmarks along 280, so familiar I could see them in my sleep. But in my mind, I felt I was wandering the remote Himalayas.

I thought about my grandfather Marvin Lewis, who had taught me that progress and principle were only effective when served together. We were going to have to let our values guide us.

I knew that what I was about to do was not a well-thought-out corporate strategy. It would be seen as a major escalation of what was quickly becoming a national controversy. There would be a backlash. Some people, even those I respected, would surely question whether it made sense for me to get embroiled in a political battle.

Nevertheless, I took out my phone and opened the Twitter app. I typed out a statement of 134 characters: "We are forced to dramatically reduce our investment in IN based on our employees' & customers' outrage over the Religious Freedom Bill."

I posted the tweet, and entered the fray.

In the otherwise silent cabin of my car, I could feel my heart thumping. I'd meant every word I'd written, of course, but I was just one person and Salesforce was just one company. I knew I'd have to be prepared to stand behind my not-so-thinly-veiled threat.

Okay, I asked myself, *what next?*

Within twenty-four hours, I was relieved to discover that I wouldn't be traveling this road alone, as statements similar to mine began to reverberate across the Twittersphere (although not yet from other business leaders). "We are especially concerned about how this leg-islation could affect our student-athletes and employees," the NCAA, the nonprofit college student-athlete association based in Indianapolis, said in a statement. Even Greg Ballard, the Republi-can mayor of Indianapolis, responded to the news by saying that his city "strives to be a welcoming place that attracts businesses, conventions, visitors and residents. We are a diverse city, and I want everyone who visits and lives in Indy to feel comfortable here."

Shortly thereafter, Salesforce's general counsel, Amy Weaver, and our government affairs head, Jim Green, activated a team to liaise with like-minded corporations, the state government, com-munity groups, and LGBTQ advocacy groups who wanted the law repealed or amended. They flew to Indianapolis and camped out near the Chamber of Commerce, which had become ground zero for outside advocacy groups.

If I was serious about sending a message about our values as a company, I knew I couldn't delegate this effort. So I began holding videoconferences with our employees and customers. I reached out to friends; I emailed dozens of CEOs and lobbied others over din-ner to join me in speaking out.

While I'd kicked open the door, many more people needed to enter it, and convincing them to do so wasn't easy. Although they had powerful platforms, many CEOs in 2015 were loath to wade into social issues, especially those with political undertones. Some of them never got back to me. Others chastised me for putting my own values ahead of shareholder value, and one person warned that my challenge to Indiana would put "a target on my back." Even my longtime mentor, the former U.S. secretary of state and chairman of the Joint Chiefs of Staff General Colin Powell, warned me that my advocacy might subject the company to unwanted scrutiny. "Be careful how far you climb up the tree," he told me, "because it will expose your backside." I began to worry that I'd opened myself, and the company, up to a slew of undesirable consequences.

I'll admit, I was starting to feel a bit discouraged. Then I remembered the recent events in Arkansas, where Walmart, which is headquartered in the state, and Acxiom, a company with seventeen hundred employees based there, had denounced a similar bill. Their opposition had helped prompt Arkansas governor Asa Hutchinson to urge state lawmakers to make changes, which they did.

I told the media that Governor Pence had been advocating for Salesforce to expand and invest in Indiana, but that this was something we simply couldn't do as long as the state permitted discrimination. We announced that we planned to move an annual customer event in Indianapolis to New York, sending its ten thousand participants and $8 million in spending out of the state.

In the days that followed, some politicians called me a "corporate bully" bent on using economic blackmail to disrupt the democratic process. Several shareholders and customers told us they were selling our stock or ditching our software.

Then, little by little, other business leaders began stepping over the threshold. Yelp Inc.'s Jeremy Stoppelman thanked me for "creating aircover for the rest of us, so we can feel OK about speaking out."

Susan Wojcicki, the CEO of YouTube and a Salesforce board member, supported me too, and Apple CEO Tim Cook published an op-ed in *The Washington Post* saying that "America's business community recognized a long time ago that discrimination, in all its forms, is bad for business" and encouraged others to stand up and oppose such legislation.

Levi's, Gap, PayPal, Twitter, Eli Lilly, and others soon joined the chorus calling on the governor to repeal the law, while mayors and governors from all over the country enacted bans on official travel to Indiana. And the indie rock band Wilco canceled an upcoming Indianapolis tour date.

A few days later, I was at the gym when my phone rang. "The governor of Indiana is on the phone for you," said a voice on the other end.

Then the governor picked up. "Marc, what's going on?"

After thanking Governor Pence for calling, I decided to dive in. "You've got to change this law, or we will bring a rolling thunder of economic consequences against the state of Indiana," I told him.

From there, our conversation grew tense. The governor asked me what "we"—by which he meant the loose consortium of Fortune 500 companies that opposed the bill—were going to do next.

"How do we work together to solve this issue?" he asked.

I explained that our only goal was to ensure equality for all people. If Indiana simply committed itself to treating everyone the same, the opposition would vanish. It was as simple as that.

On March 31, six tumultuous days after he'd signed that discriminatory bill into law, Governor Pence held a televised press conference. "We've got a perception problem," he acknowledged. Two days later, he signed a revised bill with language that made it clear business owners could not use the law as justification to discriminate based on a customer's sexual orientation.

Although we'd clearly won, I can't say we "celebrated" the outcome. I would have preferred that this fight had never happened, but I was proud of the way our employees had mobilized at every level. For the first time, I saw the full significance of the culture we'd built. It felt like a major fork in the road for the company and also for my role as its CEO.

Our employees had essentially tested me. They needed to know that I was willing to stand on principle, no matter the consequences, so they could feel protected and free to bring their authentic selves to work.

As it turned out, the Indiana fracas didn't bruise our business in the least. To the contrary: In the months that followed, Salesforce continued to post record earnings and growth. If anything, we'd actually raised our profile by inserting ourselves into the center of a national conversation about American social justice and values.

At the time, my conviction frightened a lot of people. Many in business, and especially on Wall Street, preferred to think that a CEO's responsibilities ended at the furthest edge of the corporate campus, and that all corporate leaders should limit themselves, at least publicly, to discussing matters of business.

Thankfully, that's beginning to change. In recent years, more and more leaders have begun talking about problems greater than profit and loss. Apple CEO Tim Cook, Merck CEO Kenneth Frazier, Bank of America CEO Brian Moynihan, and many other chief executives are leading with values and embracing social purpose as part of their business, as did Unilever's Paul Polman and PepsiCo's Indra Nooyi during their tenures as CEO. Larry Fink, the chairman and CEO of BlackRock, the world's largest investment firm with $6 trillion under management, has been an outspoken supporter of this new philosophy; in 2018, he informed employees that each company his firm invests in must "not only deliver financial performance, but also show how it makes a positive contribution to society."

But let me be clear: What Indiana ultimately showed me is that no one person is in charge of the moral compass of a business. The phone calls and messages from my employees proved that if the leadership won't act, they'll have to face the bayonets poking up from below. Gone are the days when companies can recruit and retain top talent without upholding a commitment to values.

In the coming era of business for good, everyone who taps their alarm button in the morning and heads to work can play a role. This isn't just a matter of what the C-suite does. It's about what happens on the shop floor or in the rows of office cubicles. Just as CEOs can't look away when social issues clash with their values, employees can't pretend that whatever its leadership decides to do is above their pay grade. If leadership won't act on a company's values, employees at every level need to hold them accountable.

In the past, having a conscience was something most people would categorize on a company's balance sheet as "other." But that's no longer the case. No business will succeed in the future until it embraces the notion that values *create* value.

We Call Them Trailblazers

In 2016, I asked Adam Seligman and Sarah Franklin, the leaders of our developer relations team, to plan a spring event for some of our most advanced Salesforce practitioners, the folks who learn to master our software and implement it inside their own companies. Even though they don't work for us, these practitioners are cherished members of our team. They are some of the greatest innovators and evangelists. Not just for our products, but for our culture.

For Adam and Sarah, the first task in planning an event for these practitioners and brand ambassadors was to come up with a name for it. "What do I call these people?" I asked during a meeting with senior executives.

We debated this for a while but remained deadlocked. Then Sarah spoke up. "We call them trailblazers," she said.

The word didn't grab me right away. I knew we had developed the Trailhead online training program, but I was more concerned with capturing the spirit of this community than I was with convenient branding. On the other hand, I wasn't on the ground working with these people day in and day out. I didn't understand them as fully as Sarah did.

The next day, with the name still undecided, Sarah sent me an email I'll never forget, because it contained the best encapsulation I've ever read of the mindset leaders need to expect, and harness, in their teams and organizations. "They want to learn, to better the world, they aren't afraid to explore, they crave innovation and enjoy solving problems and also giving back," Sarah wrote. "They are people that care about culture and diversity. They are trailblazers." I was convinced.

To my astonishment, the word "trailblazer" caught fire among our extended family of employees, customers, and partners, to the point that we quickly exhausted the supply of black hoodies we'd made with the term emblazoned on the front. I even used "Trailblazer" as the theme of my next keynote speech at Dreamforce, the annual blowout software conference we host in San Francisco.

But the trailblazer mindset isn't confined to technology, or software. Trailblazers are people like Sarah: people with ideas and convictions, who aren't afraid to voice them. They are people like Scott McCorkle, who ring the alarm bell when they see others being discriminated against or threatened. They are people like the untold number of employees, customers, and even competitors who supported our stance in Indiana because they could plainly see that intolerance and fear are the enemy of progress and profit. They are anyone in any field, industry, or company anywhere in the world who believes they have a role to play in building a better future.

Before the leadership challenges that encouraged me to write this book became urgent imperatives, I thought I understood Salesforce. The outsize response to that single word was the first clue that our business model, our values, and our founding focus on giving back had become a collective mindset—that liberated people from merely accepting the state of the world as it currently was. The determination of the people in our orbit to hike through wild, untrammeled territory without a map was changing companies, and the world around them. Trailblazers had become the focal point of our culture.

In years to come, the principles we live by, and how we discuss them and apply them, will be the essential function of any thriving business. Not because acting as responsible corporate citizens is the right thing to do, but because consumers demand it.

I realize that this is a pretty heady concept. It's probably not what you'd expect to learn in business school. So in the next few chapters, I'll show you precisely how Salesforce's values, and our community of trailblazers, have influenced its business results, how I came to understand that no matter what your company does or who your customers are, true value comes down to one thing: remembering what you stand for.

I think it's only proper to begin with *trust*.

THREE

TRUST

The Number One Value

My long personal relationship with Toyota dates back to 1982, when I used the money from the videogames I'd written as a teenager to buy my first car: a black Supra.

Back then, my appreciation for the company centered on this machine's fetching, angular lines and the seductive noises it made when I stomped on the gas pedal. In time, my fascination with Toyota only grew, although it became less visceral and more intellectual.

The source of that transition was the company's unparalleled reputation for quality and reliability. This led to astonishing success in conquering the U.S. auto market, which it achieved by adopting a complete commitment to *kaizen,* a philosophy of continuous improvement. As I studied business and launched my own career, I set out to learn all I could about Toyota, and I closely watched the rise of its CEO, Akio Toyoda, the grandson of the founder. I quickly developed a deep admiration for the company, particularly Toyoda-san's motto and all that it stood for: "There is no best, only better."

So it was with a heavy heart that I sat down on February 5,

2010, to watch a press conference that had been hastily convened near Toyota's headquarters in Nagoya, Japan. What transpired was unprecedented in the company's seventy-three-year history.

Toyota had recently surpassed General Motors as the world's largest automaker. But just as the company and its CEO should have been celebrating this long-sought achievement, they instead faced a series of disturbing safety recalls, including evidence of defective accelerator pedals. Worse, news reports suggested Toyota had been slow to act even after it understood the extent of the problems, and had attracted the scrutiny of U.S. regulators. Toyota's hard-earned reputation for quality was eroding before the world's eyes.

On its face, this was a standard cautionary tale for companies that pursue ambitious sales targets above all else. If I learned one thing from observing how my father ran his business, it's that it is never a good strategy to disappoint your customers. When you make a product that your customers rely on to safely transport themselves and their families to work, school, soccer practice, and the grocery store, the absolute last thing you want to lose is their faith. Toyota had built its reputation on values, and the most important one of all was *trust*.

As the founder's grandson, Toyoda-san took the recall of at least 8 million vehicles—and all of the fierce criticism it generated—personally. At the press conference, he told the gaggle of reporters that he "deeply regretted" the concerns these problems had caused people, and assured them that it was his "personal responsibility" to fix the situation. Then he bowed in apology.

I recognized the significance of this humble gesture immediately. Loss of face, symbolized by such a bow, is a powerful cultural totem in Japan—a tradition embodied by samurai and military leaders who, when defeated or facing a loss of personal honor, fell on their swords. I could tell his apology was heartfelt. I also knew it wouldn't be enough.

Every CEO has to perform a delicate dance between two priorities: trust and growth. Intellectually, we all know that whenever growth is put before trust, a problem will eventually appear. It can happen to the best of leaders, and to the most respected of companies. Speaking before the U.S. Congress, Toyoda-san acknowledged it plainly: "We pursued growth over the speed at which we were able to develop our people and our organization, and we should be sincerely mindful of that."

When a crisis of this magnitude occurs, it's usually a sign that the CEO has to reset the company's values and, beyond that, make sure the message cascades down into every level of the company. If the CEO doesn't make this shift, then he or she is unlikely to remain CEO for long. Toyoda-san never wavered in his commitment to fix this situation quickly. "My name is on every car. You have my personal commitment that Toyota will work vigorously and unceasingly to restore the trust of our customers," he told Congress.

As I watched these proceedings, live, from my living room, the seed of an idea began to take form.

I made my first visit to Japan during my go-go years at Oracle, where I was tasked with introducing new products that I had designed expressly for the Japanese market. It was also the period in my life when I was struggling to find meaning in my work.

At the time, I was barely pushing thirty and my well-paying Silicon Valley tech job looked plenty good from the outside. To my eyes, however, the sheen had begun to wear off. I'd started to dream about pursuing a larger purpose.

Whenever I touched down in Japan, I felt a heightened sense of clarity, along with an immediate desire to reinvigorate and reinspire myself. To this day there is something about the atmosphere on those magical islands to which I'm deeply connected. So it's no coincidence that when I decided to explore the teachings of Zen, I bought a train ticket to Kyoto.

It was there, at the Ryoan-ji temple in the northwest part of the city, that I began a lifelong journey toward developing a "beginner's mind," or what the Japanese call *shoshin*. (I'll talk more about this later on.) I began to make annual trips, often inviting friends to join me. I relished introducing them to the Japanese way of life.

Part of the allure of Japan for me is how its companies have a knack for creating brilliant, efficient, and beautiful things, from mass-market products like cars and cameras to designer T-shirts, food, and fine art. It's a country that treasures masters of innovation and design. So it should come as no great surprise that one year after we founded Salesforce, Tokyo became the location of our first office outside the United States.

In those early days, the fact that I loved going there was icing on the cake. Japan also represented a seemingly limitless market for our business. Over the years, Salesforce had picked up many prominent Japanese customers, including Canon and Japan Post. Toyota wasn't yet a big customer of ours, but I desperately wanted them to be. I was confident that Salesforce had the right products to help the company repair its relationship with customers. I let my Japan team know that I was formulating some ideas in case we ever landed a meeting. I never imagined that opportunity would so quickly arrive.

About a year after the recall, we finally booked a meeting with Toyoda-san and his top executive team. They had been visiting the United States for the Detroit Auto Show and planned to make a stop at the Salesforce office in San Francisco before heading home. It's an understatement to say I was excited—it's not every day you get to meet one of your business heroes.

There was only one problem. On the date of Toyoda-san's proposed visit, I had scheduled a family vacation in Hawaii. Disappointing my wife and kids by hopping on a plane back to California wasn't an option, so with genuine personal regret I declined.

Incredibly, Toyoda-san agreed to fly to Hawaii. Unbeknownst to me, he had a house just a short distance from mine. Deep down,

I suppose I realized that in order to convince him that we could help him win back the trust of his customers, I first needed to win *his* trust. And where better to do it than on the serene island of Hawaii, where I always felt the most peaceful and centered? Clearly this was meant to be, I thought.

For days on end, I'd been scribbling down ideas on scraps of paper only to wad them up and toss them out. I asked myself over and over, *What would be most useful to a global company struggling to win back its customers' confidence after a once-unthinkable crisis?*

What Toyota needed now, I believed, was a new vision for how it connected with its customers. It needed to find a way to restore, and strengthen, these emotional bonds, to invoke that visceral thrill and sense of connection that my teenage self had felt the first time I got behind the wheel. Suddenly, something clicked.

In 2010, we'd developed a product called Chatter, a social collaboration application for companies that leveraged features, such as profiles, status updates, groups, and real-time feeds, popularized by the consumer-oriented social networks. What if, I now wondered, we could build a social network based on Chatter that would connect drivers to the larger Toyota community in multiple ways? What if, instead of driving off the lot never to be seen until their vehicles needed servicing, Toyota's customers could feel the company's helpful presence every time they turned the ignition key? The solution, I thought, was to connect Toyota drivers, dealerships, and the mothership in ways that developed greater trust between the brand and its customers.

With only forty-eight hours until the meeting was set to begin, I called Dan Darcy, who had worked with me on some of the largest and most transformative projects Salesforce had ever executed. He brought the sales team together to create a live demonstration and build a slide deck to show how this concept could work.

Apart from our ambitious proposal, we needed to create a welcoming atmosphere for our guests. With the knowledge that gift giving is highly prized in Japanese culture, I asked a local artist to paint Toyoda-san a custom surfboard, with a scene of the Pacific Ocean flanked by local Hawaiian flowers and trees. We also arranged to have flowered Hawaiian shorts, T-shirts, and flip-flops delivered to the airport where our Toyota guests would be landing.

The weather forecast had called for rain, but on the morning of the meeting I was grateful to see it hadn't materialized. It turned out to be a gorgeous, picture-perfect, sun-drenched day. I dressed in white linen pants and a yellow shirt patterned (I couldn't help myself) with Hawaiian flowers. Then I waited.

When I opened my front door, Toyoda-san and I bowed as we shook hands. Incredibly, he and his entourage had come dressed in the casual attire I'd sent them. It was quite the scene: Executives who ran one of the world's largest companies had shed their typical attire of impeccably tailored suits and freshly shined shoes and were dressed to hit the surf.

There was instant rapport, and Toyoda-san and I quickly settled into my dining room as our teams got situated around us, taking in the view. I'll admit, sitting in my home by the beach, with the Pacific Ocean as the backdrop, was just a little more relaxing than some conference room in a skyscraper. I felt that a layer of formality had lifted, and hoped that that would help them give our ideas a more open, thoughtful hearing.

As we looked out at the ocean that separates our two countries, I told Toyoda-san about my love for Japan, and about my fond memories behind the wheel of my black Supra. I didn't do this to curry favor or to stroke his ego. I think anyone who's been in business a long time knows that relationships in business are just like those in life, in the sense that it's all about connection, not transaction. Business is temporal, but relationships are eternal. Which means they have to be genuine, and built on common ground.

Then I shared our idea. "Picture a car that has a trusted relationship with its owner," I began. "One that tells its owner when a tire is low, and where the next gas station is, and when it's time for a tune-up. But it's much more. It can help customers forge more trusted, personalized relationships with the company, *and* with its network of dealers and mechanics, and even with other drivers."

At first, Toyoda-san seemed unsure, and understandably so. He'd spent years at the forefront of automotive technology, but he wasn't a digital native. "I'm encountering a social network for the first time," he admitted. "What do you call it?"

"A car should be like a trusted friend," I said. "So we call it Toyota Friend."

Toyoda-san smiled back. "Can we take that name?" he asked.

"Hai," I answered affirmatively, in Japanese.

Toyota Friend resonated deeply with my guests that day, and before they left, we had happily committed to build it with them. The concept was ahead of its time, and it took many years for the company to fully integrate technology from us and other companies to achieve the vision. But once they did, it soon became clear that the idea had been the right one—over the next few years, other major automakers copied it or came up with their own versions. Today Toyota's five thousand stores and 280 dealership companies are using Salesforce to shift from a car-centric to a customer-centric model that engenders trust.

Personally, the most gratifying for me is the fact that Toyoda-san and I became lifelong friends. Over the years, we got together during several of my trips to Japan, and he graciously agreed to speak at some of our Salesforce events. It wasn't just any product or technology that created that bond. Trust brought us—and our companies—together.

Today that crisis seems a distant memory. Toyota is once again one of the most trusted and admired brands in the world. And what led the company back was the same value that got it there in the first place.

Warts and All

In the fall of 2018, I flew to Detroit to attend a meeting of The Business Council, an organization that brings CEOs together to share best practices and to kick around challenging new ideas. It didn't take long for the conversation to come around to a familiar topic: the erosion of trust across many institutions. This trend wasn't a new revelation to the executives of the Fortune 100 companies gathered there, but it had risen to an unprecedented level of urgency.

According to the 2018 Edelman Trust Barometer, a survey that covered twenty-eight countries and queried more than thirty thousand people, nearly 70 percent identified building trust as a CEO's number one job, ahead of producing high-quality products and services. Nearly two-thirds said they believed that CEOs should take the lead on policy changes instead of waiting for government to act. Obviously, I agreed. (The more recent 2019 Edelman Trust Barometer found an even greater percentage of respondents, 76 percent, expect CEOs to take a stand on challenging issues as well as demonstrate their personal commitment inside and outside the company. And 75 percent said they trust their employers to do what is right, significantly more than any other institution.)

This data was not surprising given the recent headlines. Wells Fargo had conceded that it had rewarded employees for opening accounts for customers who hadn't requested them, and didn't need them, and that it had billed those customers for fees on unwanted insurance and residential mortgage services. Uber had taken heat for a number of sexual assault accusations involving its drivers, and a woman engineer who formerly worked at the company had come forward with reports of sexual harassment and a toxic, dysfunctional culture that was hostile to women—the fallout from which cost founder and CEO Travis Kalanick his job. Each week seemed to bring a new revelation that Facebook had violated the trust of the 2 billion people populating its unbounded virtual universe in spectacular ways, culminating in a scandal involving Russian attempts to meddle in U.S. elections. Meanwhile top executives had tried to dismiss or diminish these problems and deflect blame.

In Detroit, we discussed how talent is fleeing many companies because they believe those companies' actions are in conflict, or out of alignment, both with their own values and the values the businesses attempt to project. The bottom line is that people want to work for employers who strive to create purposeful platforms for good. This isn't some intellectual construct. When bright employees see misalignment with their values, they view it as a personal betrayal—and then they walk.

Meanwhile, this very scenario was playing out in a loud, public fashion at Google's offices around the world, where thousands of far-flung employees had organized a walkout to protest the company's paying millions of dollars in exit packages to male executives accused of sexual misconduct.

Google has always been one of the brightest lights of the technology industry. It's well known to be a place where many of the most talented, ambitious people want to work, and where they are handsomely compensated for doing so. To me, the lesson has always been clear: No company, no matter how venerated or beloved, can afford to become complacent when it comes to trust. And that work needs to begin *inside* your company.

When we first introduced Chatter, our internal social network, some senior managers thought it was a bad idea. While it would clearly make collaboration and coordination across distance and departments simpler, some feared that it would also give employees a megaphone with which to gripe with their colleagues about problems at the company. Chatter, the naysayers reasoned, would surely backfire on us.

They were right on the first point: People would gripe. Straight away, a number of Salesforce employees formed an internal Chatter group called Airing of Grievances, which was exactly what it sounds like. I didn't know this subgroup existed until one of my executives came to my office one day in a cold sweat. It seemed that some of the conversations happening on Chatter were painting a not-so-flattering picture of the company. I asked him to display Chatter on the big screen in my office so I could get a good look at what was happening.

I don't think my reaction was quite the one he expected. "This is great!" I exclaimed giddily.

At that moment, I'm pretty sure he thought I had lost my mind. But I believed that as a leader, you need to be a lot more concerned about what people *aren't* saying than about what they are. In fact, it's when people *stop* griping that you need to worry, because that's the first sign that problems are getting swept under the rug.

Most of the grievances aired on Chatter were not exactly Code Orange. Like *There's a truck hogging a parking space,* or *The cashew bin at the snack station is empty.* But there were also important insights that forced us to reexamine long-held practices.

One of the first significant grievances had to do with the company's onboarding process. Apparently, new hires were less than thrilled with it. The thread was flooded with complaints from new hires about laptops that hadn't arrived, phones that weren't connected, missing ID badges, and so on. The tipping point was when a new employee quit on her first day. A consensus emerged that our onboarding process was akin to "hazing," and we knew we had to fix the problem immediately. For a company that had added ten thousand employees in a single two-year stretch, onboarding was mission-critical.

So we revamped the entire process to make it less erratic and more consistent, while also increasing the amount of personalized, one-on-one attention for every individual employee. Just like that, the volume of complaints trailed off.

At many companies, decisions are made behind the soundproof

doors of boardrooms. If it goes too far, secrecy at the top can make employees feel as if the company's most important initiatives are being directed by some mysterious puppetmaster. I don't believe this makes anybody especially eager to implement them.

So at Salesforce, we actually livestream our annual executive offsites so every employee in the company can watch. We also set aside time to field questions from employees. As you might imagine, this isn't exactly bingeworthy television. Not everyone bothers to tune in. What we can't measure is the value of people simply knowing that they can.

The funny thing about values is that their impact is not always quantifiable—even for a company as obsessed with data as we are. When people have a good experience, they're not even aware that in a parallel universe, it might have been a bad one. There's no way to tabulate how much lost productivity we headed off by fixing the onboarding system, or how many bright employees we prevented from leaving. I'm not saying that having to wait an extra day for a laptop would have caused people to up and quit on the spot. However, I do believe that even a small whiff of distrust, even if it only registers in an employee's subconscious, can lie dormant for months or even years, reemerging only when they're presented with a flattering outside job offer.

If there's any data of value to be mined from all of this, it's that transparency isn't about what we gain, but what we avoid losing.

Maybe I've taken transparency a bit too far at times. I know I sometimes embarrass people with my candor. Finding the right balance is not easy. Sometimes it can be downright frightening. But once you've genuinely embraced the notion of total transparency, it also becomes liberating. It starts to permeate every decision you make. It starts to lessen the destructive notion of "us" versus "them." It overcomes and exposes hidden agendas and encourages positive, ethical behavior.

It becomes, in short, a competitive advantage.

Vulnerability Makes You Stronger

Compared to Google or Facebook, or many other Fortune 500 companies, Salesforce is not a household name. We don't have stores or engage directly with consumers. We don't make smart-phones or flat-screen TVs emblazoned with our logo. I'm sure that to many of you, our name blends in with that of a lot of newfangled tech companies.

Even if we're not universally known, there's no question that we've worked hard to make ourselves knowable. In fact, when we were just starting out, our very existence depended on it. When we offered our cloud service to the public, we were asking customers to trust us to safeguard not only their financial data and sales leads, but also troves of sensitive data about *their* customers. Oh, and we were also asking that they trust us to keep all this information secure in some frighteningly obscure place we called "the cloud." Today, everyone stores everything in the cloud without giving it a second thought, but back in 1999, that was a pretty radical sales pitch.

Plus, we'd built our business on a subscription model that made it painfully easy to fire us, simply by deciding not to renew our software on any given month. At the first hint that we weren't 100 percent reliable, our customers could abandon us.

In other words, we knew from the beginning that the key to our success wouldn't solely be the cleanly designed interface that made our products easy to use, or the brilliant code that made our products work. Then as now, our secret ingredient would be our customers' confidence that we would consistently deliver on each and every one of our promises.

For a tiny start-up struggling to make ends meet, though, that was easier said than done. In our early days, back when many of our systems were barely out of the beta phase, we suffered occasional system-wide glitches that either slowed down our service or knocked it completely offline. Our business was a black box, and our customers had no way of seeing what was happening behind the scenes. On any given day, logging in and trying to actually use the product was their only way of knowing whether it was working optimally, suboptimally, or not at all.

For a business that boldly promised to lead its customers into the future with its cutting-edge technology, this lack of transparency around the status of our service was a major vulnerability—and a major source of frustration for customers. When glitches occurred, we did what most companies do in these situations. We made like an ostrich, burying our heads and saying as little about it to our customers as possible. *We* knew our engineers were working around the clock to fix the issue, but we didn't think it was particularly wise to call our customers' attention to our screw-ups. Frankly, we were also embarrassed. In retrospect I suppose it's no wonder that one of our competitors, we later discovered, had signed up for a free Salesforce trial so it could report any service interruptions to the press.

One day in 2005, during an offsite meeting with top management, my co-founder Parker Harris was in the middle of a presentation when one of his staffers rushed in to interrupt him with an urgent message. The expression on Parker's face as he read the note told me everything I needed to know. My fears were confirmed when he paused, looked out at the room, and uttered the words no CEO ever wants to hear: "Our site is down."

It took Parker's team ninety minutes to get things up and running, which was a pretty impressive feat given the circumstances. To our customers who were calling and emailing frantically and receiving no acceptable answers from us, however, it had seemed like an eternity. Trying to return to the day's stated business was fruitless. We understood that this had been a wake-up call, telling us it was finally time to trade in that black box for a clear, transparent one. After all, how long could we continue to hide from all the customers clamoring for answers?

That's when Parker spoke up and proposed a bold solution. "Let's tell everyone exactly what's happening in real time," he said.

Straight away, many executives pushed back. "Why should we show the entire world our vulnerabilities?" they asked. At first, I agreed with them. I didn't like the idea of creating some interface that allowed anyone with a laptop anywhere in the world to monitor our service disruptions. It seemed like corporate suicide.

Within minutes, though, I started to see it differently. Sure, the easiest thing to do was *nothing;* to just sit back, clench our teeth, and wait for the issue to be resolved. The bold, counterintuitive, and quite possibly correct move was to embrace radical accountability: to let our customers see what was happening, warts and all.

Long story short, that's how trust.salesforce.com came into being. To this day, the site provides real-time information on our system performance, scheduled maintenance, transaction volume and speed, and any and all security issues. And over time, we've let our customers in on more and more of what was going on behind the scenes of the company, from sharing our proprietary plans for new product rollouts well in advance so they could plan for them, to previewing the content ahead of our annual Dreamforce conference.

I won't try to deny that when you put yourself out there, there's usually some pain involved. Vulnerability is scary. But it also makes you stronger.

Awesome, Guaranteed

January 9, 2007, was a date that tech and gadget enthusiasts recall with the same reverence as the 1969 moon landing. It was, of course, the birthday of the iPhone.

To the many industry insiders who watched Steve Jobs unveil this world-altering device at the Macworld convention in San Francisco, the iPhone's significance wasn't immediately clear. But I just knew in my gut that the future had arrived. Soon everyone in the world would be carrying these devices, which weren't really phones but powerful miniature computers, in their purses and pockets.

I realized that many of these people would be Salesforce customers, and these people would want the ability to run our software on these sleek devices. Parker, who attended this event with me, had the same reaction. He called the iPhone "earth-shattering." And he was right.

The next day, I went in to work and announced the pivot to end all pivots. From that moment forward, I told my team, we'd be redirecting our engineering resources to a new goal: turning Salesforce from a desktop company into a mobile one. Mobile functionality would have to be infused into every single product we made.

If you'd told me, that day, that this system-wide, all-hands undertaking would require us to completely rethink the way our engineering teams approached their work, I would have been terrified, though not completely surprised. With technology advancing at a blistering pace, what got you *here,* as they say, isn't what will get you *there.* As Parker told the engineering team, "Let's forget all the old versions. It's no longer a new version of Salesforce. It's a new vision." What I didn't anticipate at the time is how it would test our resolve and the culture of trust we had built over the years.

As soon as Parker and our engineering team launched this campaign, they experienced one failure after another. To work on mobile devices, the software we'd built to run on desktop computers had to be reconfigured with an entirely new technical architecture. The problem: None of us had been trained to do this. None of us even had any deep knowledge of how to build simple software that took advantage of a touch-screen interface.

Our first development sprint, monumental as it felt for us, produced a mobile app that our customers basically hated. They complained that it was too clunky and slow. This failure, on top of many others, had hacked away at our morale and confidence. Fortunately, we knew enough about innovation to understand that you can't use the same approach and expect a different result. So we decided it was time to shake things up.

In 2012 Parker began looking for a new mobile team leader, and he settled on Srini Tallapragada, who had led large engineering teams at two of our competitors, Oracle and SAP, and was universally respected across the industry. Shortly after Srini arrived, I called a special meeting of my core management team to rethink our mobile plan. As we went around the table in my office, several executives offered detailed suggestions. When Srini's turn came, however, the newcomer had only five simple words: "It will be awesome, guaranteed."

Everyone laughed at his expression of bravado, including me, but the impact it had was remarkable. The room seemed suddenly re-energized. And when the mobile team got wind of what their new boss had said to the big boss, they loved the fact that Srini had stuck his neck out so boldly. They trusted him immediately.

One of the first changes Parker and Srini made had nothing to do with writing code. They removed the entire mobile team from their modern new offices in the Landmark building across from San Francisco's iconic Ferry Building and installed them back into the same inferior space they'd recently abandoned a few blocks away. The engineers weren't exactly thrilled about being exiled to this desolate workspace with peeling paint and no views, amenities, or furniture, but Srini insisted. He knew that sometimes, to see a problem in a new way, you need a change of scenery. Or in this case, a lack of scenery.

In Silicon Valley, the concept of continuous iteration—focusing on making small, incremental improvements to what you've already tried—is practically a religion. Until then, we'd been loyal disciples. Each time a version of our mobile app failed, we'd iterate endlessly, holding out hope that these small corrections would add up. But they never did. And now Parker and Srini wanted their team to start over.

The team needed a morale boost. So Parker and Srini rolled out the office whiteboard on which Parker scrawled, in big, colorful letters: AWESOME, GUARANTEED. Of course, the engineers didn't feel their work was awesome at the time. Nonetheless, every one of them took a leap of faith and signed it.

The mobile team worked long days in their dreary war room. It was exhausting, and exhilarating at the same time. At one point, they began building a new app from scratch. In the final stages of coding, some forty engineers—including Srini—worked through the night. The team spirit they built on this project lasts to this day.

In May 2014, and after several grueling years of fits and false starts, our vision for a mobile version of Salesforce had been realized. The Salesforce1 Mobile app set the standard for enterprise mobility, winning us scores of new customers, including companies like Philips and Stanley Black & Decker, whose employees were freed from having to be constantly tethered to their desks.

When the new San Francisco Salesforce Tower opened in 2018, the engineers from the mobile team hung a piece of that whiteboard in the shared space on their floor. On it were the words AWESOME, GUARANTEED.

Over the years I've learned that trust and transparency are two sides of the same coin. As CEO, I could lay all our company secrets—all our code, all our financial data, all our technical troubles—out for all our employees to see, but if those employees can't count on *one another,* no amount of openness on the part of management will be enough. The people in the trenches need to be able to trust that their team, and their leaders, will be right there on the ground, working beside them, when the going gets tough. Guaranteed.

The Deal That Never Was

Trust may seem like a simple concept, but in fact it's quite multifaceted in nature. To some extent, it's a matter of trusting others, but at the same time, it's also about ensuring that others can trust you. For a leader, the most difficult of all is knowing when it's appropriate to trust your own judgment, even when no one else around agrees with you.

As a rule, I've never been someone who spends a lot of time worrying what other people think of me. I suppose that explains why I'm sometimes caught on video dancing at courtside during Golden State Warriors basketball games, or showing up at work with Salesforce's Chief Love Officer, aka my pet golden retriever. I've always been inclined to march to the beat of my own drum, even when others might think I'm crazy. After all, I trusted myself enough to quit a great job to start a company in a small rented apartment, even after every venture capitalist in Silicon Valley told me that my idea was worthless.

I'd learned over time to trust my instincts and thought I had a pretty good track record in that regard. But it wasn't until recently that I came face-to-face with a leadership quandary unlike any I had studied in business school—a high-stakes situation that forced me to ask myself the uncomfortable question: *What if your instincts are wrong?*

At some point, every leader will find themselves taking a position that requires them to discount the judgment of all the smart people around them. Ultimately, it's going to come down to a simple choice: Do you continue to go with your gut and follow what every instinct is telling you is right, even if it may cost you the trust of the people who've helped you get where you are?

This was the very dilemma I found myself up against in 2016 when I became convinced that Salesforce ought to buy Twitter.

The business case, in my head, was a strong one. I believed that acquiring the platform would give our customers a new and versatile point of public presence. It would allow them to engage with *their* customers one-to-one and to more efficiently market, sell, and support their products. It also seemed like a brilliant way for companies to solicit candid feedback and diverse perspectives—the seedlings of innovation—on an entirely new scale.

Twitter, I knew, would also offer our customers access to a potential treasure trove of data from its more than 300 million users.

And I strongly believed that by tapping into this social platform, we, too, could vastly improve our advertising, e-commerce, and other data-rich applications. Plus, Twitter was struggling, and the way I saw it, the merging of our two companies would be beneficial for us both.

Unfortunately, however, my management team wasn't just lukewarm about the idea; their positions on the issue ranged from highly skeptical to staunchly opposed. They didn't understand how buying a distressed social network that was out of favor with many investors made any sense to our core business, which was selling software.

These concerns failed to deter me. At least at first.

Although we tried to keep our pursuit of Twitter quiet, the news eventually leaked out. The more people told me I was crazy, the more my ardor for the idea grew. I told people that Twitter was an "unpolished jewel" and a precious one at that. I even settled on a rough price I was prepared to pay for the company, upwards of $20 billion.

My team and I were still at loggerheads, and as the rumors swirled, even I began to sense that I might be sailing into the eye of a storm. Our stock price had begun to fall, and not by insignificant amounts. Apparently Wall Street didn't have much more confidence in the idea than did my team at Salesforce.

I'm not a superstitious person, but I've always believed in the power of signs and omens. Looking back, I realize that I'd become so singularly focused on winning over the naysayers that I nearly missed a big one.

That fall I scheduled a meeting with the credit ratings agencies with the intent of persuading them to give us investment-grade underwriting we'd need to make the Twitter acquisition, which would have been our largest ever. The meeting was set to take place early one morning at Salesforce headquarters, and at the appointed hour, I climbed out of my car, feeling mostly ready to make one of the biggest pitches of my career.

That's when I failed to properly judge the gradient of a curb, tripped on it, and went down *hard*.

Mark Hawkins, our chief financial officer, had been standing next to me before I tumbled. His voice was familiar, but the frantic tone was not, when I heard him yell:

"Big man down!"

Take it from me: It's one thing for a CEO to take a public spill in front of his executive team. It's another to do so on a heavily trafficked sidewalk in full view of scores of employees and just as many horrified passersby. It didn't help that I'm six feet five inches tall, either. I'm told that the thud was tremendous.

My colleagues rushed toward me, and bent down to see if I was conscious. I quickly pulled myself off the pavement and looked down at my jeans. My knee had landed on a metal plate, which ripped my pants wide open and sliced into my leg. I could feel blood oozing out, dripping down my shin. I didn't realize it at the time, but the fall had split my meniscus. *Keep going and ignore the pain,* I told myself.

"Guys, let's power on," I said out loud, as my chief of staff, Joe Poch, stared at me in disbelief.

Despite my best efforts to hide it, I was mortified. I'm not a clumsy person, and prior to that day I'd managed to step out of a vehicle and remain upright without incident for the last fifty years. Looking back, though, I don't think the timing was a coincidence. There was a lot going on in my head. My feet were telling me what my brain would not.

I made a valiant pitch to the ratings agencies that day, and I knew that they'd give me the benefit of the doubt on the transaction. But my own doubt, which had been festering silently in the furthest reaches of my mind, proved too strong in the end. Two weeks later, onstage at Dreamforce, I looked out over the worried faces of my colleagues, directors, and investors, nearly all of whom were opposed to a Salesforce-Twitter union, and decided it was time to let go. It wasn't so much about our stock price, which had continued to slip on the deal speculation, as the realization that I needed these people to trust me more than I needed to trust my own instincts. So I did something I rarely do. I apologized. And I made it clear that I had decided to walk away from the deal.

The nice thing about stumbling, figuratively and, in this case, literally, is that it always yields insight. What the Twitter incident taught me is that there are many different strains of trust, and sometimes those strains will collide. The true measure of a leader, no matter what business you're in, is whether you can navigate those collisions and come out stronger.

Whether you're starting a business, managing a team, or running an entire company, trusting your instincts can be essential in bringing a vision or idea to life. I now understand that trusting yourself is only half the story. To be effective as a leader, you need a reservoir of trust to draw from. And once you use it all up, it can take years and years to replenish.

It's possible that Salesforce lost untold billions in potential value by walking away from the Twitter deal. It's also possible that the acquisition would have destroyed the company. We will never know.

What's not included in any calculation is the value of the trust we retained.

At one of the regular dinners with entrepreneurs that I host at my house in San Francisco, I once had a long talk with a young start-up CEO. I asked him to identify his company's highest value. "Innovation," he replied, in a tone that implied the answer was obvious.

When I asked why he hadn't answered "Trust," he looked at me strangely and explained: "I just don't believe it. I believe that the best idea wins, and that's the key to Silicon Valley success."

Maybe that's how it was, once, I replied, "but it's not how it is going to be going forward." Yes, innovation is important. But when you start valuing innovation over trust, then you're really in hot water; you'll be the frog luxuriating in warm water and unable to react when it comes to a boil.

I've said it before and I'll say it again: There's no way to put a dollar value on values. And yes, there will be times when prioritizing values, especially trust, will come at the expense of profits. In the short term, that is. But the money your company makes in any given quarter will never be more valuable than the trust you stand to lose over time.

If you ask most successful CEOs, especially founders, to name the major milestones that really made their companies great, they usually settle on a story that revolves around a breakthrough product or idea. It might be a revolutionary clean-energy technology, a wildly popular accounting software program, or some small tweak to a search engine's algorithm that left the competition gasping—or anything in between.

It's not surprising that these tangible things are the ones most of us default to. Every new innovation or product has a "before and after," and the difference is something you can quantify. *Check out these sales numbers, this customer retention rate, and these earnings! Amazing!*

I wish I could tell you that I'm above getting excited about something so superficial as an eye-popping percentage increase or a hyped-up product rollout. But I've bragged many times about Salesforce's products and profits. When we figured out how to provide all of our customers with the ability to customize applications, I could have happily whipped out a chart that showed our revenue jumping 25 percent over the next fiscal year and explaining why such a gain was astounding for a company our size. It was just the kind of graphic-friendly home run we CEOs love patting ourselves on the back for.

I sincerely believe, however, that the real story of Salesforce's success is best explained by the moments when trust prevailed over stubbornness or ego—the moments when transparency triumphed over fear of embarrassment, or even the potential loss of millions of dollars in revenue.

A great product that your company builds can be like a mighty oak. It can provide everyone who planted it with a pleasing patch of shade to camp under for years. Values like trust may not make for dramatic earnings charts and they may never become the tallest trees. They are more like hundreds of small acorns you bury in the ground in the hope that they'll become saplings. If I've learned anything over the years, it's that if you nurture them, those saplings eventually grow up together. There's not a single tree on earth that's sturdier than a forest.

FOUR

CUSTOMER SUCCESS
Transformation Through Technology

When I learned that my personal financial adviser at Merrill Lynch was on the line, and that he'd described the call as "urgent," I figured that meant one of two things, neither of which was the least bit good. Either the stock market was taking a nosedive or one of my investments had flatlined.

Actually, the news was even worse than that. It was about Salesforce.

As it turned out, my adviser wasn't calling about my portfolio, but rather to warn me that my company was on the verge of losing *his* company's business. In 2013, Merrill Lynch wasn't just any Salesforce client. It was our single biggest.

Six years earlier, when Merrill decided to install Salesforce software for its twenty-two thousand client advisers, it was the first truly massive business to sign with us. At the time, I'd declared this a major coup and the surest sign yet that Salesforce was poised for growth. I'd reasoned that if this leading financial services firm trusted us to manage all their highly secure, technically sophisticated systems and transactions—in the cloud, no less!—there was nothing we couldn't do.

Now we apparently had a problem. My adviser had just stepped out of a company-wide meeting during which John Hogarty, Merrill's COO, had told thousands of advisers that the company ought to kick Salesforce to the curb—prompting the whole room to erupt in applause. "No one likes your product here," my adviser explained, unnecessarily. "You need to get involved and fix this quickly."

To make matters worse, the Merrill Lynch Mutiny of 2013 (as I've come to think of it) wasn't the result of some outside circumstances that none of us could control. The company hadn't been seduced by a competitor, or slashed its IT budget. The explanation was brutally simple: They didn't like our software.

The problem was this: Merrill's advisers, who were the guardians of its bedrock business, valued speed and functionality above all else. Salesforce software took too long, they thought, and the interfaces we'd built for them weren't intuitive or easy enough to use. Simple tasks required too many small steps, siphoning off priceless minutes from their workdays. Even something like retrieving a contact from their address books, for instance, required three clicks, each with a six-second wait time. The more I learned about the nature of their frustrations, the worse it sounded. I wasn't the least bit surprised that Merrill was livid and that we were on the verge of getting fired.

This was a dark day for me on a number of levels. Losing Merrill as a client would be a disaster in and of itself, but the ripple effects could be catastrophic. Merrill's rejection would send the message that Salesforce wasn't ready for the big leagues, prompting other important clients to dredge up their own complaints and rethink their relationships with us. Beyond that, I was furious that we hadn't been aware of these problems *before* they exploded into a five-alarm fire. Most of all, I just felt terrible that we had failed to live up to one of our core values: customer success.

At Salesforce, our mantra is that nothing is more important than giving our customers the tools and support to be successful. Sometimes it's a matter of growth, raising revenue or net profit; other times it's a matter of better reaching and connecting with their customers. Often, success simply means streamlining previously byzantine processes and operations—enabling a customer of ours to redirect more of its time and attention elsewhere. It might sound hokey, but our customers' success is how we measure our own success at Salesforce. After all, we can't grow unless our customers are growing with us.

Yet here we were at the edge of a cliff. We'd failed to uphold this value with Merrill Lynch.

Shortly after that meeting, Mark Alexander, Merrill Lynch's CIO, informed us that we'd been placed in "containment," meaning that we could conduct no further new business with the bank until we'd fixed these usability issues. By "the bank," he meant not just Merrill Lynch but also its parent company, Bank of America, one of the world's largest financial institutions. We'd already landed some business with BofA and had been working hard to win more. Losing this account might shut that door forever.

I knew my adviser was right; I had to step in and do something to address the situation—and fast. After clearing every other issue out of my brain, and off my desk, my first phone call was to Simon Mulcahy, a then forty-one-year-old London-born Salesforce executive we'd hired in 2009 to handle some of our most complex customer engineering projects. A former British Army officer, Simon had previously worked for the World Economic Forum, where he'd created an "Innovation Heatmap" that was so ingenious the Smithsonian wanted it for its collections.

So there was no one better than Simon to spearhead a "Get Well" program to put us back on track with Merrill Lynch. He joined me in San Jose for a dinner with John Thiel, head of Merrill Lynch Wealth Management, to whom I gave my word that we would fix these issues—and that Simon would have every resource necessary to do so.

Working on borrowed time, and under enormous pressure, Simon began hopscotching around the country on a grand tour of Merrill Lynch's regional offices. He'd set up meetings with several dozen advisers, who he hoped could shed more light on which features and functions of the software they (and their colleagues) hated most, and what specific improvements they hoped we could make to them.

A couple of weeks into this journey, a funny thing happened. Simon discovered that his interview-style approach wasn't yielding a lot of meaningful, actionable input. Most people in his position might have felt relieved by the fact that the majority of the advisers' complaints amounted to small, relatively simple fixes to the software. But Simon couldn't reconcile the fact that even when added together, these gripes didn't seem to explain the intensity of the advisers' frustration.

It seemed that Simon had a mystery on his hands.

When I first started working in sales for Oracle, back in the 1980s, the notion of sitting down with clients to talk about how our products were working, let alone engaging in exhaustive bouts of problem solving, was rarely top of mind. Back then, Oracle and other fast-growing companies adhered to a simple strategy that went like this: "See a bear, shoot a bear." In other words, if you were meeting with a customer, your singular goal was to leave the room with a signed contract—in as short a time as possible.

I'd never been a fan of this strategy. The problem was, it didn't incentivize anyone to consider whether the customers on the other side of these transactions really needed the software they had purchased, or whether it helped them make progress on their own business goals. And it didn't leave a whole lot of time to build trust, either.

When we founded Salesforce, I vowed to avoid that business model as much as possible. There were only a few companies selling enterprise products back then, and all of them required customers to lock into long-term contracts with hefty maintenance fees. If you didn't like the results, in other words, you were pretty much stuck. So with Salesforce, we decided to sell subscriptions that could be canceled at any point, which meant that it didn't matter how many bear pelts we collected. Our renewal rate became the measure of whether or not customers were getting what they needed from our software, and thus it also became our chief barometer of health.

It took a while to get this formula right. In the beginning, our customers were mostly small businesses who paid us monthly on their credit cards and could cancel at a moment's notice. After a while, I realized we had an attrition problem, and we needed to make a fundamental shift in our operational philosophy. We weren't about to turn our back on our fundamental business model, so we had to reorient our efforts to show our customers that our mutual interests were aligned—that our success depended on how quickly they achieved their own.

Our first step was to offer customers another point of contact beyond the sales department—a person whose job it was to listen, rather than to close deals. We created a team of customer success managers whose entire function was to understand how customers were using our software tools and, if they decided to bail on us, to circle back and find out why.

Over time, our team of customer success managers continued to grow in importance, and in number. They became so much more than glorified customer service reps: They were the eyes and ears of our company, collecting the invaluable feedback that we used to not just improve our products, but also to tailor those improvements to the specific and unique needs of our customers.

In 2013, however, this system seemed to have fallen short. Merrill Lynch was so big, and its needs so specific, complex, and difficult to articulate, that we hadn't been able to see that our products weren't getting the job done.

By this point, Salesforce was fourteen years old and our engineering team had become a formidable force. We were confident that we had enough programming firepower to fix whatever was wrong. But even as Simon took meeting after meeting with Merrill's advisers, he was still having a hard time figuring out exactly what the problems were, let alone what needed to be done to solve them.

Simon began to get the feeling that the advisers were only telling us a partial story. He had noticed that Merrill's advisers had plenty to say about the small glitches, like address book navigation, that they thought we should be able to fix. What they weren't talking about were the big, sweeping improvements that could fundamentally transform how they did their jobs—because they simply didn't realize that our software might have the power to solve them.

So Simon decided to pivot. He tucked the script of questions he'd been asking back into his briefcase and started opening meetings by asking the advisers to forget about software for a second. He invited them to pull the camera back from the minutiae of their workflow and show him a more panoramic, zoomed-out view of the larger challenges they faced in their work. Now, finally, the truth began to emerge. For example, when they asked for faster speed in navigation, what they really needed was smarter "tasks" that could do things like triggering proactive alerts about their clients and guiding them to useful market data.

When Simon told me about how this approach had immediately started generating scores of promising ideas, it reminded me of a quote attributed to my boyhood hero, Albert Einstein: "If I had an hour to solve a problem, I'd spend fifty-five minutes thinking about the problem and five minutes thinking about solutions."

In the end, Einstein was right. If you focus the bulk of your time and effort on understanding the problems, solving them becomes the easy part. In the past, we'd been trying to help our customers simplify or automate all of the small, tedious business functions that ate away their time. That was important, but in a world where technology holds almost limitless possibilities, marginal improvements couldn't come at the expense of stepping back and identifying the biggest, most urgent and potentially painful challenges our customers faced, and then figuring out how to address them.

It's hard to overstate how important this shift would turn out to be. It allowed us to see that the real problem wasn't the software we'd built for Merrill. It was the customer success infrastructure we'd built. What Merrill's advisers showed us is that we were going about the process backwards.

By tackling the problems behind the problems, we could engineer the software to make our customers more efficient in ways they couldn't have imagined. From that point forward, we knew we had to stop focusing on checking off boxes and start trying to figure out how to deliver breakthroughs.

This philosophy isn't just applicable to the software business, or even to the technology world. Any company can provide its customers with features that can make them more successful than they ever thought they could be. They just have to stop shooting bears and start listening for what their customers really need.

Dreamforce and the Power of Community

Salesforce was one of the first companies to make "customer success" a stated value, but we always knew the job didn't end there. After all, values aren't worth much unless they translate into behavior and are brought to life.

One of the tactics we've used to animate the principle of customer success might seem elaborate, or even moderately to highly outrageous: We made it the focus of a conference that has become an annual festival.

If you happen to live in the Bay Area, you are likely familiar with this spectacle. Every fall, more than 170,000 members of Salesforce's extended family of employees, customers, practitioners, independent software developers, partners, and investors from ninety countries register to visit San Francisco and are joined by another 15 million people who follow the proceedings online. We call this event Dreamforce.

Dreamforce is often described as a software conference, and I guess that's accurate. We're definitely a software company, and we do hold scores of seminars, product demonstrations, and other conference-like fare. When we launched Dreamforce, the idea was to bring lots of our customers to our home base all at once, to showcase our new products and generate more business. But many of our participants prefer to describe it as a family reunion, and while that may sound a little exaggerated, it's equally fitting. A lot of people come to Dreamforce to see old friends, to meet new ones, and to revel in the feeling of community.

To some extent, it's a four-day opportunity to consider big ideas and pursue better versions of ourselves. We've had keynotes by Michelle Obama, Melinda Gates, and Jeb Bush. We host a CEO series where business leaders discuss everything from women's leadership to equality, sustainability, and mindfulness. We've invited Al Gore to deliver a lecture on confronting the climate crisis, Congressman John Lewis to talk about advancing equality, and Oscar-winning actress Patricia Arquette to talk about equal pay. Participants can join daily meditation sessions led by saffron-robed Buddhist monks.

On some level, it's also a blowout party. Participants organize big, boisterous dinners at San Francisco restaurants, and we've hosted concerts by Stevie Wonder, U2, Lady Antebellum, Neil Young, and the Foo Fighters.

The way I think of it, Dreamforce is where Salesforce comes

alive, a place where people come together under the umbrella of our shared values to mix and mingle, eat and drink, meet and share learnings with interesting people in many different fields. No two people come for the same reasons or leave with the same feelings about what the gathering meant to them.

When we held our first Dreamforce in 2003, we had no idea how many people would sign up. At the time we had fewer than four hundred employees and just eight thousand paying customers. I remember telling our conference chair, Elizabeth Pinkham, to lower the ticket price because I was afraid no one would come. I asked her to pull two hundred chairs from the main auditorium just to avoid the embarrassing spectacle of empty seats. "I want it to look like standing room only," I told her. Needless to say, I was overjoyed when more than a thousand people showed up.

Today, we cordon off the streets surrounding the Moscone Center to accommodate our "Dreampark" campus, where we lay down AstroTurf for an entire city block; erect climbing walls and waterfalls; have a dozen bands perform in rotation on an outdoor stage; and set up picnic tables piled high with boxed lunches that our busy participants can grab as they race between activities. Events, meetups, and happy hours spill out into dozens of hotels and restaurants in the city's South of Market, Financial District, and Union Square neighborhoods. I can barely find a moment to sleep while Dreamforce is going on, and I still don't manage to experience the full breadth of what's happening there. One year, turnout was so high that we partnered with Celebrity Cruises, who docked a ship we called the *Dreamboat* in San Francisco harbor to house all the participants that local hotels or Airbnb hosts couldn't handle.

It never ceases to amaze me when the tactics you employ to meet one goal evolve to serve another. What started as an opportunity to sell more software has become the embodiment of an idea: putting the customer at the center of everything we do. In fact, the larger Dreamforce has gotten, the less it has become about us. Today it's a celebration of our customers, a place where they come to revel in their success, acquire new skills, study broader trends in technology and innovation, and discuss social issues. These trail-blazers aren't just thinking of their own success; they want to inspire *others* to take their businesses, and their careers, to another level. This is why many of the twenty-seven hundred educational sessions and workshops are actually led by customers rather than employees, and why some customers have begun organizing their own affinity groups and events, or even hosting their own Dreamforce-related podcasts.

In other words, Dreamforce isn't about bolstering our bottom line, it's about helping our customers to continue making progress in a world that's continuously being disrupted by advancements in the cloud, mobile technology, social media, and artificial intelligence. It's hard to describe the combination of joy and purpose our participants radiate while they're dashing around the campus, soaking up all the learning they can and sharing their discoveries with one another. It's a strange, sometimes wacky energy field where our community's trailblazing spirit comes to life.

A few weeks before Dreamforce 2016, I hosted a dinner at the Westin Hotel in Times Square in New York. I wanted to deliver a preview of my keynote address to a handpicked group of customers and skilled practitioners of our technology. They ranged from CEOs of large financial firms to Salesforce evangelists from every level of their companies. The dinner was meant to be a fun way of thanking them for their loyalty and support, but it was also an opportunity to get some feedback on a speech I was about to deliver to thousands of people.

The main topic of my Dreamforce keynote was a new product called Einstein, which would allow our customers to tap into the increasingly sophisticated artificial intelligence capabilities we'd been building into our software (you'll read more about it in Chapter Five). I was ecstatic about its impending launch, and I hoped my guests would be swept away by my boundless enthusiasm. When I finished my dress rehearsal, I opened up the floor.

"You are our focus group," I said. "Tell me what you think."

The response wasn't the one I'd expected. Nobody wanted to talk about my keynote, or about Einstein. They weren't really interested in talking about software at all. What they really wanted to discuss was how excited they were to head to San Francisco in a few weeks to reunite with friends and colleagues at Dreamforce, and what new knowledge they might be able to absorb there.

It dawned on me then that whatever was transpiring inside Salesforce's engineering laboratories paled in significance compared to what was going on outside them. Dreamforce was the focal point of a community: one comprised of bright, engaged, ambitious people coming together to prepare themselves for the challenges and opportunities of the future. They came to make progress and celebrate their accomplishments, but they came to celebrate one another's progress and accomplishments as well.

Today, if I'm talking to the leaders of a company and they don't seem to be buying my arguments about the value of values, I explain how Dreamforce is the ultimate expression of our brand and customer success, and how our community inspires and creates a virtuous circle of growth. People who become successful using our products want others to join them, and in turn, our community and our business grow.

Connection, on Every Level

As the global financial crisis erupted in 2008, many Salesforce customers faced a reckoning they'd long dreaded. The era of easy money and aggressive expansion vanished, quite literally overnight. The best many executives could do was tread water and pray they could manage to stay afloat until things returned to normal.

Even as the economy began to bounce back, however, many of our customers knew intuitively that the notion of "normalcy" had to be reevaluated. The euphoria of the roaring economy had given them permission to keep pursuing familiar old business models. Yet the moment that narcotic wore off, they faced a second frightening fact: Technology was coming for them. The skies had begun to clear, but we at Salesforce saw a new set of clouds looming menacingly on the horizon. Many of our customers were about to be at a critical infection point. Home Depot was one of them.

Ever since Bernie Marcus and Arthur Blank dreamed up the idea for a one-stop shop for home improvement supplies at a Los Angeles coffee shop in 1978, the company had been a high-flying and highly profitable phenomenon. Its big-box stores with bright orange signs brought convenience and order to the disparate, sclerotic supply chain that had long frustrated contractors and homeowners. It also harnessed, and likely accelerated, a major socioeconomic shift: The strong economy, combined with easy credit, not only fueled a massive housing boom, it also turned millions of Americans into home-improvement junkies. TV shows about buying, renovating, and flipping houses began dominating the ratings, earning Home Depot an enviable position at the center of the zeitgeist.

Home Depot was hardly the only Salesforce customer popping champagne as the housing bubble kept on growing. But the Great Recession left it with a hangover that was worse than most. Plunging home prices, tightening credit markets, and disappearing jobs brought its expansion to a screeching halt. People had lost all enthusiasm for renovating their homes. They just hoped to hold on to them.

After Lehman Brothers collapsed in September 2008, triggering a massive stock market dive, Home Depot's chief financial officer ordered its store managers to transfer all of their cash—every crinkled bill in every register and safe across the country—to Atlanta headquarters. Over the next several months, the company did everything it could to make that cash last: slashing all capital spending, freezing plans to open new stores, halting its stock buy-back program, closing three major divisions, and laying off seven thousand employees.

Home Depot's sprawling stores and giant inventory, once their greatest competitive advantage, suddenly became their biggest liability. The aisles and parking lots that had once been bustling were now virtually empty. Sales suffered double-digit drops, and thousands of orange-aproned sales associates who'd built up years of expertise and close customer relationships were rendered expensively idle. Worse yet, Home Depot could hear the ominous footsteps of online retail giants like Amazon challenging them with their impossibly low prices. Like many brick-and-mortar retailers, Home Depot began to suspect that some customers were using their stores as product showrooms and their employees as consultants, then driving home and buying what they needed online.

At Salesforce, Home Depot's predicament was a source of grave concern. Since the company became a customer in 2007, we'd worked with them with some smaller projects at the margins while suggesting grander ones. We wanted to help Home Depot prepare for the wave of digital disruption that was about to upend retail. Now was not the time, executives told us. The company wanted nothing to do with any new spending.

In 2011, the market had finally begun to come up for air, but it was clear that the economic recovery wouldn't compensate for all the sales migrating online. We knew that if Home Depot was to have a strong future, it needed to embrace a digital strategy.

Even before the Merrill debacle, we'd believed that it's every Salesforce employee's job to listen to our customers—to try to understand what they actually need, rather than pitching them our latest products and trying to maximize sales. To do this well, we're often forced to step away from our desks and walk in a customer's shoes. That goes for the CEO, too.

So in 2011, I decided to get involved personally on Home

Depot. I worked with our Salesforce office in Atlanta to hammer out a plan, then flew out to present it to Home Depot's executives. My goal was to inspire a mindset shift. I wanted to convince them that technology could be a savior, rather than a death sentence.

As we rode to the meeting, Warren Wick, the head of Salesforce's big accounts in Atlanta, felt optimistic. Home Depot's defensive plays had started to pay off, he said. Finally, they were ready to go on offense. As we pulled past security in the parking lot, however, we both fell silent when the guard referred to the corporate headquarters as the "Store Support Center." That told me everything I needed to know. Clearly, Home Depot still thought its future rested with just its physical big-box stores, when it should have been embracing a digital strategy where customer support could occur online.

"At Home Depot," Warren explained, confirming my worst fear, "the mindset is all about the stores."

"Do they realize Amazon has *no* stores?" I replied.

We had to convince Home Depot to put its community—not physical stores—at the center of its culture.

Technology can be disruptive. Thousands of companies live in fear of being "Ubered" or "Amazoned," and in many cases, rightly so. But at the same time, technology has incredible value to connect and empower your customers. That was exactly what Home Depot needed to do, and I believed that Salesforce's engineers could deliver the perfect software for the job.

The challenge was bigger than we thought. The company didn't even have a customer database. "We still need a whole lot of help in the technology area," Matt Carey, the chief information officer, told me. Yet the problem wasn't the technology per se. It was missing the opportunity for a multifaceted relationship with their customer.

We proposed that Home Depot invest in the success of the homeowners and contractors it serves. That meant providing them a way to get the tools, materials, and advice they needed to complete a job, not just by visiting the orange-aproned representative in the store, but also by logging in online from the comfort of their home or job site.

It was a pretty simple idea, really, I told Matt: "What you need is a new way to build a deep connection at every possible level."

We built a software application that linked up its hyper-knowledgeable orange-aproned associates all over the country, allowing them to consult one another instantly on mobile devices. If a customer had a question they couldn't answer or an item they couldn't find, or if an associate wanted to consult with or offer guidance to colleagues, they could type a few lines and *voilà*!

Home Depot's new Warehouse application grew rapidly. By 2018, this hive mind had 190,000 active users and 2 million posts per month. When a customer walked inside one of the company's cavernous stores, they knew they were almost certain to get the answers they needed to fulfill whatever vision they had for their project. Over time, contractors and homeowners stopped treating Home Depot as a glorified showroom and began to see it as a welcoming community of knowledgeable associates willing and able to help them pick out the perfect paint color, the best washing machine, or the right power tools to get a job done.

Eventually Salesforce helped Home Depot establish one-stop resources for customers embarking on DIY projects like remodeling their kitchen, as well as a system for placing orders with contractors to oversee renovations like gutting an old home or installing a new toilet.

In 2014, Home Depot finally stopped treading water. The company defied all expectations, not to mention the trajectories of most big-box retailers, by undergoing a serious growth spurt. Thanks largely to its burgeoning online retail business, the company's share price more than doubled over the next four years. In 2017, *Fast Company* named the retailer one of the world's most innovative companies.

The secret to Home Depot's success was combining its physical locations with its online services to create the community experience that customers really wanted.

Home Depot's business used to hinge on how many drill bits and sheets of drywall it pushed through the checkout lanes. By linking its far-flung associates wirelessly, and connecting consumers and contractors as well, Home Depot realized that technology was not the enemy.

I can't put a dollar value on the pride a customer feels opening a bottle of wine inside the beautiful new gazebo she built, or the sigh of relief a contractor breathes when he gets a tough job done not only on time, but under budget. What I *can* tell you is that Home Depot changed the narrative. It stopped viewing technology as a threat but rather, as Matt described it, as a tool to help *its own customers* feel understood, connected, cared for. And when it succeeded, so did we.

Success, Redefined

Over the years, Salesforce has benefited from some favorable, well-timed tailwinds. One of them, undoubtedly, is the shift to online commerce and the increasing emphasis companies are placing on the digital customer experience.

By 2013, the fledgling industry we'd gambled on back in 1999—customer relationship management, or CRM—had become the largest and fastest-growing software segment in the industry. After all, every company with products to sell saw the need to take friction out of their online customer interactions, and this necessity had rippled outwards up from sales departments and IT to just about every business unit.

At the time, though, I couldn't have known that the customer success philosophy would soon be a boardroom topic. And it's not only relevant in industries like ours that are primarily devoted to serving other businesses. "Customer success" has become a buzz-word in every sector, from transportation and entertainment to re-tail and financial services.

Nothing a company does is more essential than how it engages with customers. In a world where online portals are replacing cus-tomer service centers and algorithms are replacing humans on the front lines, companies like ours continually need to show that the personal connections our customers craved were still—and always would be—there. I don't just mean connections with our sales reps or customer success managers, but with the CEO, too.

Even now that I run a company of more than forty thousand employees, I've never forgotten what I learned from my dad: Noth-ing can take the place of human relationships, the bedrock of any business. In 2013, we realized that as we were gaining more and more business around the world, I would need to bring on another executive—someone who shared the company's values and who could work with me to connect with customers on that human level.

For years, I'd been trying to bring Keith Block to Salesforce. And now I decided it was time to pursue him with everything I had. Keith and I got hired at Oracle around the same time, but we worked on different coasts and didn't know each other well. He had stayed for more than two decades, most recently as a top ex-ecutive building up their enterprise business. I knew that he was the rare sort of person who could "speak the language of the cus-tomer" and help us in the next phase of growth.

Around the time we were working on our Merrill Lynch "Get Well" program, I asked Keith to breakfast in San Francisco. Keith hails from Boston, so naturally we kicked off our meeting with an impassioned discussion of our respective hometown teams: his Pa-triots and Red Sox and my Golden State Warriors and Giants. Then, for the next two hours, we exchanged our views on innova-tion, company culture, and of course, customer success.

Keith had studied information systems and management science at Carnegie Mellon, and his perspective on these subjects was deep, and eye-opening. I could also tell that his East Coast professionalism and measured demeanor would be a nice complement to my California vibe and outgoing personality. Once I discovered that he owned a Hawaiian shirt (a sartorial favorite of mine), I knew the stars had aligned.

Shortly thereafter, Keith became our new president and then chief operating officer. It's hardly a secret that talent is the foundation that any great company is built upon, but it's hard to overstate how strong a pillar this one particular hire would turn out to be. As Salesforce expanded its portfolio of products beyond sales and service to include marketing, analytics, AI, and more, Keith helped us expand our footprint into financial services, healthcare, retail, and other kinds of diverse businesses all over the world.

I now know that adding Keith to the team made our customers more successful because it helped the entire company better meet their needs. Turns out that customer success isn't just a virtuous cycle; it's also a two-way street.

A Mile in Their Shoes

When I think back to our near disaster with Merrill Lynch, I can't forget something Ulrik Nehammer, the former chief executive of Coca-Cola Germany, once told me, shortly before he came to work at Salesforce. "The most dangerous place to make decisions is in the office," he said. "You need to make decisions where the customer is."

Which is why, for the final phase of our "Get Well" campaign, Simon's army of engineers basically moved into Merrill's offices and camped out next to the advisers as they worked. This extremely close proximity allowed them to address the deeper software problems we'd already uncovered *and* root out new gremlins. It also enabled them to tinker with solutions on the spot, and then gauge the advisers' reactions.

In September 2014, roughly a year after the first alarm bells were sounded, we rolled out a new console to all of Merrill Lynch's advisers, who by then numbered twenty-five thousand. We gave them a whole new way of calendaring and scheduling, we simplified how they captured notes and created tasks, we even introduced a new search paradigm. Within months, adoption of our platform inside the company climbed from 60 percent to 90 percent. Soon we were out of "containment" and back in their good graces.

It's possible that we could have saved our Merrill account by micromanaging the problem and doing just enough to quell their frustration. That certainly would have been easier. Instead, we attacked the problem by remembering what we aspire to become and being unafraid to reconsider the methods that worked for us in the past.

It felt great to win back their business, but for me, what felt even better was the perfect synergy our values had created: prioritizing "customer success" won us back Merrill's trust, while also fostering new solutions and innovations. The crisis also gave us a new blueprint for how to troubleshoot with our customers, and a useful reminder that success is not a matter of doing just enough to keep a customer's business, it's about giving customers the tools they need to succeed—both now and in the years ahead.

These learnings would prove useful when a new customer soon came to us with a problem of a different kind.

It was Kasper Rørsted, CEO of Adidas, who told us that his multinational sportswear brand was trying to get a handle on the emerging generation of shoe buyers. These people were digital natives who expected "instant gratification," he explained, and Adidas was facing considerable pressure to ensure they received it. Too often, online customers were seeing the words "come back later," or worse, "site down," flash across their screens when they visited the Adidas site. When the company offered a limited number of pairs of its wildly popular Kanye West "Yeezy" shoes for sale online, for one day only, the volume of traffic crashed the site, embarrassing the company, alienating its customers, and even straining its relationship with Kanye. Adidas needed to transform its entire customer experience, eliminating the kind of friction that turned people into critics rather than evangelists.

Adidas knew the next Yeezy shoe would be huge. The demand was already there. Success, as Adidas defined it, was a matter of providing a transaction experience that would live up to customer expectations and build personalized connections with hundreds of millions of fans.

We worked with Adidas to make sure the platform could handle a high number of simultaneous visitors, as well as weed out the hacker bots that manipulated the system to buy Yeezys and other hot items in bulk for resale. We were able to handle the technical issues pretty quickly, helping Adidas achieve a record holiday season's one-day sale, while creating a digital community around the brand.

The larger strategic challenge Adidas faced, however, was parlaying product demand into more lasting relationships with its customers. The company needed a better way to keep sneaker fanatics engaged with its website more frequently, in higher numbers, flash sale or no flash sale.

Before writing a single line of code, we all ordered sneakers with Adidas's signature three-stripes logo. We'd always talked about the importance of walking a mile in a customer's shoes, so here was our chance to actually do so. With my size-14 Pharrell Williams Adidas sneakers on my feet, I rounded up some of our best engineers and data scientists and told them all that they were going to be embedded at Adidas headquarters. It wasn't long before Salesforce's then chief product officer, Alex Dayon, pulled into Adidas headquarters with an eighteen-wheeler filled with demos and robots to demonstrate how artificial intelligence could help the company get to know its customers better and engage with them like never before.

An AI-powered website could analyze the data stored on past purchases and use it to personalize every customer interaction by predicting which styles each shopper would want and directing them to special offers. These intelligent product recommendations would help customers find exactly what they wanted.

In November 2017, Adidas launched an AI-powered app built with Salesforce that by spring 2019 had been downloaded more than seven million times in more than twenty-five countries. In 2018, the company's online revenue skyrocketed 36 percent.

The success Adidas achieved was our success as well. We listened to them, absorbed their culture, and understood what they really needed. That's how we partnered with them to achieve it.

As I write this, I know there are countless mysteries about the future of business that we've yet to unravel. That's a process that will never end. When it comes to customer success, however, I have achieved absolute clarity on four points.

First, technology will never stop evolving. In the years to come, machine learning and artificial intelligence will probably make or break your business. Success will involve using these tools to understand your customers like never before so that you can deliver more intelligent, personalized experiences.

The second point is this: We've never had a better set of tools to help meet every possible standard of success, whether it's finding a better way to match investment opportunities with interested clients, or making customers feel thrilled about the experience of renovating their home.

The third point is that customer success depends on every stakeholder. By that I mean employees who feel engaged and responsible and are growing their careers in an environment that allows them to do their best work—and this applies to *all* employees, from the interns to the CEO. The same goes for partners working to design and implement customer solutions, as well as our communities, which provide the schools, hospitals, parks, and other facilities to support us all.

The fourth and most important point is this: The gap between what customers really want from businesses and what's actually possible is vanishing rapidly. And that's going to change everything. The future isn't about learning to be better at doing what we already do, it's about how far we can stretch the boundaries of our imagination.

The ability to produce success stories that weren't possible a few years ago, to help customers thrive in dramatic new ways—that is going to become a driver of growth for any successful company. I believe we're entering a new age in which customers will increasingly expect miracles from you. If you don't value putting the customer at the center of everything you do, then you are going to fall behind.

Whether you make cars, solar panels, television programs, or anything else, untold opportunities exist. Every company should invest in helping its customers find new destinations, and in blazing new trails to reach them.

To do so, we have to resist the urge to make quick, marginal improvements and spend more time listening *deeply* to what customers really want, even if they're not fully aware of it yet. In the end, it's a matter of accepting that your success is inextricably linked to theirs.

FIVE

INNOVATION

Artificial Intelligence and the
Power of Ecosystems

In the summer of 2015, a dozen rock-star engineers at Salesforce received a meeting invitation from me. The subject line consisted of just two capital letters: *AI.*

As the engineers arrived and took their seats around the conference table, I could tell they already had a pretty good idea of what was about to happen. I had called them together to announce that we were launching a companywide project to infuse AI into every product in our portfolio. And their job was to figure out how to harness all the talent in the company to do it.

No pressure or anything.

If the microprocessor was the defining technology of the late twentieth century, artificial intelligence and machine learning were, by every conceivable measure, poised to become the signature advancements of the twenty-first. Soon the most important functions of our lives, not to mention the future success of Salesforce and its customers, would depend on our ability to swim with these invisible currents. We didn't want to be late to the revolution.

When I gathered our engineers that day, AI was still in its em-
bryonic phase, yet it had already been adapted to perform a host of
specialized tasks, like predictive searches on Google, fraud detec-
tion at financial institutions, real-time language translation, and
surfacing the most adorable cat videos. First-generation AI-powered
devices like Apple's Siri and Amazon's Alexa were up and running;
answering questions like "What's the weather?" or "What's on my
calendar this morning?" activating home appliances on-command,
storing information like shopping and to-do lists, and continuously
correlating between thousands of variables to help make future interactions "smarter."

As cutting-edge as these applications seemed, we all knew they
held vast potential that we hadn't even begun to imagine. Whether
in the cloud or in our pockets, computers had become so powerful—
and generated such massive amounts of data—that breakthroughs
in machine learning wouldn't just alter the playing field; they would
change the game entirely. And it would happen fast. Soon our customers would be pleading with us to lead them into this new frontier. As my co-founder Parker Harris put it, "AI will have more
impact than the Internet. We are still in the first inning of this
game."

The great promise of AI was that for the first time companies
could turn the troves of data they'd acquired on consumer behavior, industry trends, demographic shifts, and more to start uncover-
ing patterns that human brains couldn't detect. These capabilities
would only become more sophisticated as machines became smarter
and smarter, and they could soon be used to tailor communications
with exacting precision: everything from the best time to contact a
customer, to the right subject line to use in an email, to what features or qualities to emphasize when describing products on social
media. In other words, AI could take everything it "understood"
about the past and use it to make astonishingly accurate predictions about the future. If we tapped its full potential, we knew it

could generate intelligence and insights that would help our customers succeed in ways they never thought possible.

The most exciting promise of AI wasn't the ability to do any one thing more efficiently; it was the tantalizing possibility of doing almost *everything* better. This vast potential was also what made AI so daunting. We didn't have anything even resembling a blueprint, let alone a plan of action. We knew we wanted to build an AI tool for business: one that each individual customer could easily customize using clicks, not code, and one that could handle billions of customer interactions on desktops and smartphones. But given that no one had built such a tool before, we had no idea how we would go about it.

All of the time we'd invested in leveraging the quantum leaps in computing power and developing more sophisticated algorithms to collect and make sense of customer data had been a prelude to this. If AI could be applied effectively and ethically, we knew it could do incredible things. We also knew our livelihood as a company depended on it.

For many, the term "innovation" has become almost synonymous with Silicon Valley, and not without reason. After all, so many iconic technology companies—Hewlett-Packard, Intel, Apple, Oracle, Cisco, Intuit, and Google, to name a few—were born there. It's where thousands of start-ups still plant their roots each year in hopes of becoming part of the legend, and its spirit has been imported to scores of enterprising cities around the world. Not everyone who dreams of building "the next big thing" makes it. But some do.

Growing up in close proximity to this storied place, I've watched technology change the landscape; both literally, as farmland and apricot orchards gave way to microchip plants, and virtually, as the region became the hub of vast invisible networks connecting billions of far-flung people around the world.

As I've watched the region evolve over time—witnessing so many once-promising companies run out of cash and disappear, so many talented entrepreneurs burn out, and the company logo atop so many office buildings get swapped out as its occupants change—I've also learned how easy it is to become a footnote to history. To weather the winds of change constantly blowing through Silicon Valley—and anywhere else big things are happening—it's not enough to just talk about innovation. If you don't *value* innovation as a foundational principle, you will never achieve it.

I don't think it's possible to estimate the total amount of time we've spent discussing innovation inside Salesforce. Of all our core values, it's the one that seems to correlate most quantifiably to traditional measures of business success. That's why we'd hired the brightest talent, and then nurtured it by harnessing creativity inside our walls. Because for any business, and certainly any technology business, the line between innovation and metrics like stock price, revenue, and profit is a pretty straight one.

Successful companies continuously innovate, period.

That day in 2015, as I sat around the table with my top engineers, I knew I was tasking them with an ambitious challenge—perhaps the most ambitious in our company's history. I also knew the stakes were high. It wasn't just the question of whether Salesforce would have a future in AI that was on the line. It was whether we would have a future.

I was confident that our team could deliver. After all, they'd already weathered so many challenges, somehow figuring out how to weave together the cloud, social networks, and mobile into our CRM apps. At the same time, I also knew that AI was the tallest mountain we'd ever tried to scale.

One thing I've learned about high-stakes business initiatives is that they're essentially a stress test. They'll always tempt you to question your values, and maybe even loosen your grip on them. But often, they'll also lead to new and eye-opening insights that only drill those values even deeper into your culture.

That meeting in 2015 wasn't a particularly long one. We went over some of the AI applications we thought were promising, and brainstormed some possible new directions to pursue. My team and I already knew this challenge would force us to walk our talk on innovation. What we couldn't immediately see is that to do so, we would need to reinvent our approach. We were going to have to do more than simply round up our best people, give them a deadline, and send them off to work. As we were about to learn, meeting this challenge would require a certain form of courage.

I ended the meeting by circling a date on the calendar: the kick-off of Dreamforce 2016. We would have less than a year to get our first ever AI product off the ground.

We'd had ample time to study. AI was our final exam.

"Be Mindful, and Project the Future"

The first great role model in my life, aside from my father and grandfather, was Albert Einstein.

He was a genius, of course. One of the greatest innovators of all time, he quite literally unlocked the secrets of the universe. But that wasn't all. As an advocate for social justice who campaigned tirelessly against the use and proliferation of nuclear weapons, he also exemplified what it means to live and work by your values, just as my grandfather had done.

Beyond all that, he still managed to approach his work with a passion that bordered on childlike wonder. "Imagination," he is said to have observed, "is the highest form of research."

To me, Einstein's rare combination of knowledge, moral conviction, intuition, and insatiable curiosity represented an almost impossible ideal. Like the Zen Buddhists who inspired me later on,

Einstein was able to let go of preconceived notions and think about the world in an unconstrained way. This spirit was the one I'd eventually aspire to re-create inside Salesforce.

As a teenager, I hung a poster of Einstein in my bedroom and convinced my high school math teacher to hang another in his classroom. In a classic case of youthful adulation (and perhaps a touch of hubris), I quoted the great man in my Burlingame High School senior yearbook: "Great spirits have always encountered violent opposition from mediocre minds."

When we set up Salesforce's first office in a San Francisco rental apartment, it was under Einstein's watchful gaze that we worked ourselves ragged day and night. My co-founders—Parker Harris, Dave Moellenhoff, and Frank Dominguez—and I weren't trying to codify the laws of physics, but we were dead set on disrupting the software industry and proving the doubters wrong.

Of course, I'm hardly the only Einstein acolyte in my line of work. After all, those who dream of becoming the innovators of the future can't help but pay homage to the great innovators who came before them.

This may explain why my next greatest role model was none other than the legendary Steve Jobs.

I first met Steve in 1984 when Apple hired me as a summer intern. The fact that I'd landed this gig in the first place was something of a fluke; as a college student at USC, I'd reached out to the company's Macintosh team to complain about a bug in its software and somehow parlayed that conversation into a job. While I'd done my best to impersonate a seasoned developer, at nineteen years old, the sum total of my programming experience was writing a dozen arcade and adventure games in high school. Working at Apple was the big leagues, and while I felt profoundly underqualified, nobody tossed me out the door that summer. In fact, every time Steve Jobs passed my cubicle, I somehow summoned the nerve to strike up a conversation.

It wasn't much, but through those small interactions, a bond would eventually form. Steve and I shared a love for technology and science as well as a passion for meditation and Eastern philosophy. In addition to being a brilliant executive and peerless innovator, he was a spiritual, intuitive person who had a gift for seeing the world through many perspectives at once. I saw that he had a willingness to share his wisdom, and I wasn't afraid to ask for it.

Even once my internship ended, we stayed in touch, and as my career progressed he became a mentor of sorts. Which is why, one memorable day in 2003, I found myself pacing anxiously in the reception area of Apple's headquarters.

In the four years since Salesforce opened for business, we'd hired four hundred employees, generated more than $50 million in annual revenue, and were laying the groundwork for an IPO the following year. We were justifiably proud of our progress, but I'd learned enough about the technology business to know that pride is a dangerous state of mind.

Truth be told, I was feeling stuck. To catapult the company into the next phase of growth, we needed to make a bold move. We'd survived the scary start-up phase where so many companies crash and burn, but I was struggling to imagine how I'd navigate the pressure of running a public company that has to lay itself bare to Wall Street every quarter.

Sometimes seeking guidance from mentors is the only sure way to survive these bouts of inertia. That's why I decided to make a pilgrimage to Cupertino.

As Steve's staff ushered me into Apple's boardroom that day, I felt a rush of excitement coursing through my jangling nerves. In that moment, I remembered what it had felt like to be an inexperienced intern mustering up the courage to say a few words to the big boss. After several minutes, Steve charged in, predictably dressed in his standard attire of jeans and a black mock turtleneck. I hadn't settled on precisely what I wanted to ask him, but I knew I'd better cut to the chase. He was a busy man, and was legendary for his directness, and ability to quickly zero in on what's important.

So I showed him a demo of the Salesforce CRM service on my laptop and, true to form, he immediately had some thoughts. After unleashing a torrent of rapid-fire suggestions on our software's basic functionality, down to the shape and color of its navigation tabs, Steve sat back, folded his hands together, and got to the larger point. Salesforce had created a "fantastic enterprise website," he told me. But both he and I knew that that alone wasn't enough.

"Marc," he said. "If you want to be a great CEO, be mindful and project the future."

I nodded, perhaps a bit disappointed. He'd given me similar advice before, but he wasn't finished.

Steve then told me we needed to land a big account, and to grow "10x in twenty-four months or you'll be dead." I gulped. Then he said something less alarming, but more puzzling: We needed an "application ecosystem."

I understood that to hit the big leagues, we needed a huge marquee customer win. But what would a Salesforce "application ecosystem" look like? Steve told me that was up to me to figure out.

By January 2006, Salesforce had topped $300 million in revenue, tripling in size in the three years since that meeting. We were growing fast, but the more innovative products and features we released, the more our customers expected from us. Our engineering team, brilliant as they were, had begun to bump against the upper boundary of its productivity. Privately, I started to worry about whether we could cope with the pressures of scaling up.

In previous eras, a company in our position would have tapped its most brilliant scientists and squirreled them away behind a triple-bolted door with TOP SECRET painted on it. These appointed geniuses would have spent long days in isolation, wrenching together prototypes and puzzling over clay models, walled off from any ambient noise. Back then, the prevailing model for innovation was secretive, expensive, and time-consuming. Outside input was decidedly unwelcome.

At the end of the process, these scientists would emerge from their lairs, likely overcaffeinated and unkempt, and would wheel out a gurney containing some new product, the likes of which nobody had ever seen. Then it was up to customers to determine whether it was a game changer. Too often, it wasn't.

We had subscribed to this outdated model too, in the early years of the company. Then, in 2006, the approach to innovation at Salesforce started to change. This wasn't a conscious decision, or something we spent a lot of time planning for; it was almost purely a response to the challenge we were up against. To innovate on a truly massive scale, we realized that we couldn't simply demand more of our already overworked engineering department. The only possible way to scale up our innovation efforts was to start recruiting outsiders.

One of the unique things about this digital era is that it operates through a very different type of infrastructure: the common language of computer programming. You can't build automobiles without a factory, but if you are a developer fluent in the language of programming, all you need is source code to build a new application. Every year, the global army of talented developers was growing. All we had to do, I suddenly realized, was harness that talent, and we could produce as many shiny new cars as we wanted.

One evening, over dinner in San Francisco, I was struck by an irresistibly simple idea. What if any developer from anywhere in the world could create their own application for the Salesforce platform? And what if we offered to store these apps in an online directory that allowed any Salesforce user to download them? I wouldn't say this idea felt entirely comfortable. After all, I'd grown up with the old view of innovation as something that should happen within the four walls of our offices. According to this view, opening our products to outside tinkering was akin to giving our intellectual property away. Plus, it would involve letting go of the controls, which felt like the polar opposite of leadership. Yet, at that moment, I knew in my gut that if Salesforce was to become the new kind of company I wanted it to be, we would need to *seek innovation everywhere.*

So I sketched out my idea on a restaurant napkin. And the very next morning, I went to our legal team and asked them to register the domain for "AppStore.com" and buy the trademark for "App Store."

Shortly thereafter, I learned that our customers didn't like the name "App Store." In fact, they hated it. So I reluctantly conceded and about a year later, we introduced "AppExchange": the first business software marketplace of its kind, and the first major initiative born out of our new commitment to seek innovation everywhere.

About two years after we launched AppExchange, I returned to Apple's Cupertino headquarters in 2008 to watch Steve unveil the company's next great innovation engine: the sprawling, boundary-less digital hub where millions of customers, developers, and partners could create their own applications to run on Apple devices. Steve was a master showman, and this presentation didn't disappoint. At the climactic moment, he said four words that nearly floored me: "I give you App Store!"

All of my executives gasped. When I'd met with Steve Jobs in 2003, I already knew he was playing a hundred chess moves ahead of me. None of us could believe that Steve had landed on the same name I'd originally proposed for our business software exchange.

For me, it was exciting and humbling. And Steve had unwittingly given me an incredible opportunity to repay him for the prescient advice he'd given me five years earlier. After the presentation, I pulled him aside and told him we owned the domain and trademark for "App Store" and that we would be happy and honored to sign over the rights to him for free.

By 2019, AppExchange had more than five thousand apps available for purchase, ranging from sales engagement and project management tools to collaboration aids. And nearly 90 percent of Salesforce customers were using them.

Steve helped me understand that no great innovation in business ever happens in a vacuum. They're all built on the backs of hundreds of smaller breakthroughs and insights—which can come from literally anywhere. Building an ecosystem is about acknowledging that the next game-changing innovation may come from a brilliant technologist and mentor based in Silicon Valley, or it may come from a novice programmer based halfway around the world. This principle applies to technology, of course, but it applies to intellectual, scientific, and theoretical breakthroughs as well.

Whether in the business of software, retail, arts and culture, or anything else, a company seeking to achieve true scale needs to seek innovation beyond its own four walls and tap into the entire universe of knowledge and creativity out there.

Innovation, Everywhere

In 2014, Salesforce purchased a company called RelateIQ, whose software captured data from users' email, calendars, smartphone calls, and social media posts and used it to provide important insights and reminders. If a sales rep hadn't heard back from a customer, for instance, the software would put all the relevant variables together—like the date of their initial meeting and the dates of all prior correspondence by both phone and email—and automatically generate a task reminding the sales rep to follow up. At the time, it was the closest thing we had come to building AI capabilities into our software. We knew it was the kind of practical and predictive intelligence we needed to spread across our business.

When I announced our big AI initiative a year later, one of our first projects had to do with a problem that our sales team had been describing in feedback sessions for years: They were desperate for a tool to help them prioritize their efforts so they could stop spending too much time on accounts that never bore fruit.

So a small group of data scientists led by Hernan Asorey took on the challenge, and they built a system of "opportunity scoring." Essentially, the algorithm looked at variables such as length of time a sales opportunity had been in play, how many competitors were going after the same account, the dollar value of the account, and the account team behind it. Then it would generate an opportunity rating of one to five stars. By tracking the outcome against its own predictions, the algorithm could get smarter over time and make better suggestions in the future.

This tool was a huge hit with our sales team, who saw a productivity boost right away. So in the summer of 2016, we made opportunity scoring available to some of our customers as well. We still had quite a bit of distance to travel before that Dreamforce 2016 kickoff date, but we were on our way.

This was around the time I decided that our AI campaign needed a name. This might sound trivial, given everything else we still had to accomplish, but we couldn't go around calling it "the AI project" forever; it needed an identity. I thought it should be something dramatic and recognizable, like IBM's Watson. Not surprisingly, I made a plea for "Einstein." It was too fitting to resist: "Salesforce Einstein, the world's smartest CRM!" Plus, to build Einstein the machine, we'd have to channel the spirit of Einstein the man.

In the months leading up to Einstein's scheduled debut at Dreamforce 2016, a small team, lead by engineers John Ball, Vitaly Gordon, and Shubha Nabar, worked around the clock from a cavernous office space beneath the West Elm furniture store in downtown Palo Alto, where they had decamped to get away from the distractions of Salesforce headquarters.

But as it turned out, even those brilliant minds in that improvised laboratory would need to seek innovation outside its four walls.

Hernan had worked at Salesforce since 2014 in the important, though not exactly flashy, role of employing data to understand how our customers use every single software product. Then he applied those learnings to guide product decisions about which new features and releases to invest the most money in, based on customer adoption and market trends.

One of the great things about embracing innovation as a core value and creating a strong ecosystem to feed it is that everybody at every level of Salesforce is encouraged to share new ideas. At Salesforce, we believe that a good idea is a good idea, period, no matter where it comes from. As a result, everyone from the summer interns to the senior management can feel confident that their ideas can work their way into the conversation.

Which is probably why, in early 2016, Hernan didn't hesitate to approach me to let me know that we had a problem. During a management meeting he had attended a few weeks prior, I'd asked my sales executives from various regions to forecast their numbers for the quarter. Every one of them told me that they were on target with internal projections—and yet when our numbers for the quarter came in, one of our sales execs had turned out to be dead wrong, leaving us with an unforeseen shortfall.

But Hernan wasn't just voicing his concern. He had an idea.

What if he could feed all the quarterly sales data into Einstein and build a financial forecasting tool that could get smarter and smarter as time went on? If he got the algorithms right, he figured, we would no longer need to rely on our executives to make accurate quarterly forecasts. AI would do it for us.

This was a big undertaking. And to execute it, Hernan would need to be freed up from his usual duties. This wasn't ideal, but we knew that if we were going to crack the code on AI, innovation would have to take priority over everyday products and functions. So Hernan requested and received time and resources from his boss, Alex Dayon.

It was the trailblazing spirit at its best, and Hernan pulled it off. These days, when I have my twice-monthly meeting with twenty of our top executives, Einstein is always in the room. After my executives offer their opinions and predictions about different regions, products, and opportunities, I turn to the *virtual* Einstein on my phone to see what he thinks.

Einstein then gives me its over/under prediction for the quarter, identifies where we're strong and weak, and even points out specific patterns or areas of concern. Sometimes Einstein's analysis can be painful to hear, and I'm sensitive to that. But it's rarely wrong. And beyond that, it has given us something I believe every company needs: an objective, unbiased, unemotional voice at the table.

Even though it was outside his job description, Hernan developed something that ultimately became more than just an internal tool for our sales executives. It became Einstein Forecasting, one of our hottest products. In fact, after I described it during an interview with Jim Cramer on CNBC, my phone began blowing up with calls from CEOs of companies big and small. Every one of them wanted to know if they could have Einstein Forecasting.

On September 19, 2016, we formally introduced Salesforce Einstein at Dreamforce, right on schedule. As proud as we were of this achievement, we were also aware that our work was far from done. This was the beginning of our AI journey, and we would need the full force of our ecosystem to make more progress.

A Work in Progress

One summer evening in 2018, tucked into a booth at a downtown San Francisco restaurant called Boulevard, two of Salesforce's brightest technical minds ordered a bottle of red wine and launched into one of their regular monthly strategy sessions.

This one would be devoted almost entirely to their favorite topic, AI.

Bret Taylor, our new chief product officer, and Richard Socher, our chief scientist, were already many months into the next phase of our AI initiative. Among other things, they were working building apps with deep learning capabilities that could understand anyone, no matter what language is spoken, and digital assistants that could converse, in voice and chat, in anyone's natural language. Their session on this evening was the result of ambitious acquisitions, led by John Somorjai and his team at Salesforce Ventures, the venture arm we founded in 2009 to keep an eye on emerging trends and promising start-ups as well as to extend our innovation ecosystem, fill gaps in our product technology, and find talented computer scientists just like Bret and Richard to bring in.

Bret, who is full of energy and wisdom beyond his thirty-nine years, has an incredible résumé. He had been Facebook's chief technology officer and was the engineer who came up with the iconic Like button. Prior to that, he'd been at Google, where he'd co-created Google Maps. Bret had also co-founded a start-up called Quip, which was an app that allowed real-time communication and collaboration on documents, lists, tasks, spreadsheets, and presentations, across many devices. When we bought Quip in 2016, we not only gained an amazing technologist and executive in Bret, but also a host of next-generation productivity tools that we could integrate into Salesforce's suite of products.

Richard, too, embodies the spirit of a trailblazer. A world-renowned AI researcher, he has an impish smile and mop of carrot-colored hair and is sometimes affectionately referred to as "the boy scientist." On many weekends, you'll find this thirty-six-year-old German native loading his paraglider and jet surfboard into his station wagon before heading to the Bay. To see him rev up his motor and hurtle straight into a breaking wave, you'd never guess he was a leading AI expert on deep learning—that is, on teaching software to mimic the way the neurons in our brains retain and process information. He is no slouch in the field of natural-language processing either, with more than thirty-four thousand scholarly citations to prove it.

Few people on earth, even in Silicon Valley, would have understood a fraction of the bewildering acronyms and jargon Bret and Richard tossed around that night. These accomplished innovators—along with dozens of other brilliant new hires and longer-term employees—were an embodiment of our commitment to seeking innovation everywhere.

Thanks to their collective effort, we've been able to infuse AI into our products so seamlessly that customers barely even notice it's there. Think about how effortless it is to use Amazon's Alexa, or Apple's Siri, or Google Assistant to check the weather or play music. Thanks to Qingqing Liu, our top mobile engineer, we now have something similar that can help people run their businesses. In just a few months, she took all the underlying AI technology, along with mind-blowing quantities of Salesforce data, and turned it into an amazing experience we now call Einstein Voice Assistant.

Now Einstein lives in the palm of my hand, where he functions as a voice-enabled digital assistant that understands the context of our business, attends our meetings, collects the relevant data in order to update notes and records related to the conversations, and even contributes comments. Our goal is that over time, we'll be able to provide every customer with AI-powered digital assistants like these—and that they will grow more sophisticated as the technology evolves.

In coming years, more and more innovation will come from humans and machines working together, taking advantage of the unique capabilities of each. With machines doing more of the routine, repetitive work and the pattern recognition humans can't, we'll be free to spend more time trying to "be mindful and project the future" (as a wise man once advised me to do).

There are legitimate concerns about the ethics of AI, and I share them. But in the end, it's humans who are crafting artificial intelligence, and these tools will be exactly as ethical as the people who build them. By the same token, machines don't have a beginner's mind, and no technology is either inherently good or inherently evil—what matters is how it's used. The products of the future will only be as good as the honest, open conversations that happen around them.

The fears about AI and robotic automation eliminating jobs, too, are very real. This is why I believe that as computers take on more tasks previously performed by human workers, we need to find more ways to help people continuously adopt the curious, open-minded, adventurous spirit of a trailblazer, so they can learn and adapt to this brave new world ahead.

Like it or not, artificial intelligence is our future. And the only way it will work, at Salesforce or anywhere, is if the people designing the technology collaborate seamlessly with the people using it. Which makes it all the more critical that we fully embrace the fact that innovation truly does come from anywhere.

In 2017, just a few months after joining the company, Richard Socher approached me with a worried expression. As chief scientist, he didn't understand how I expected him to do all the cutting-edge work we envisioned with the modest budget he'd been given.

"You're not spending enough money on innovation," he said with genuine puzzlement. "How can you call innovation a core value?"

At first I didn't quite understand the question. In my view, the budget was fine. Then I remembered that Richard hadn't been with us long enough to understand how innovation worked at Salesforce. He didn't realize that our ability to build innovative products wasn't solely a matter of how many dollars we threw at research and development. It was also about having a diverse ecosystem of curious people who challenged conventional wisdom and were empowered to pursue wild ideas.

Here's how we do innovation at Salesforce, I told Richard: "We seek innovation everywhere."

SIX

EQUALITY

A Good Look in the Mirror

In March 2015, when Salesforce's employee success chief, Cindy Robbins, arrived at my home for one of the regular meetings I host with my senior executives, I could tell that something was a little off. Not only did she seem oddly reserved, even a bit anxious, she'd taken the unusual step of bringing backup, namely another senior woman executive, Leyla Seka.

I've never believed that the corporate office is the best backdrop for a relaxed, candid conversation, which is why I usually convene these one-on-one meetings at my home office. The standard attire is "casual," which, in the vocabulary of tech companies, translates to "jeans." On this day, however, I had taken "casual" to a new level. As it happened, I was competing in a charity Fitbit challenge against Dell's founder and CEO Michael Dell and had waltzed into my meeting wearing shorts, a T-shirt, and a baseball cap. I could tell by the energy in the room that something important was clearly about to transpire, and I'd shown up looking like a gym rat.

Cindy and Leyla were both in their early forties and had grown up in the Bay Area. Cindy had joined Salesforce as a recruiter in 2006 and eventually rose to President and Chief People Officer, directly overseeing seven hundred employees. Leyla had signed on in 2008 as director of marketing for Salesforce AppExchange and gone on to a variety of roles in our business-software units.

Although they'd been close friends for years, they often laughed about how they hadn't meshed at first. While Cindy is a self-described introvert with a reputation inside the company as a calm and steel-spined professional, Leyla, who is as extroverted as they come, wears Birkenstock sandals with designer scarves and once worked in the Peace Corps. After getting off to a rocky start, the pair had eventually bonded over the shared challenges of climbing the ladder in a male-dominated industry.

"What's up?" I asked, tentatively.

If Cindy and Leyla were thrown off by my workout attire, they didn't show it. They sat down and got right to the point. They'd come to tell me they suspected that women employees at Salesforce were being paid less than men for the same work.

"We need to determine if pay inequality exists here," Cindy announced.

I'm sure the look on my face betrayed the mix of indignation and astonishment I was feeling. I'll admit, my defensiveness was welling up. For starters, I believed that Cindy and Leyla's mere presence undermined their point: These high-ranking and highly paid female execs were walking, talking proof of Salesforce's commitment to gender equality.

Moreover, I'd been working hard at this problem for three solid years. In 2012, I'd begun to notice, with horror, that when I called a meeting, the number of women in the room was often close to zero. I soon discovered that less than 29 percent of Salesforce's total employees were women, and they made up only 14 percent at the leadership level. To make sure talented female employees were being considered for leadership roles, I'd started an initiative I liked to call the Women's Surge. I announced that going forward, gender equality was going to be made a priority. And that from now on, at least 30 percent of the participants at any meeting, from a large management session to a small product review, should be women.

Holding equality as a value is not just a matter of fairness, or doing the right thing. Nor is it about PR, or "optics," or even my own conscience. It's a crucial part of building a good business, plain and simple. And there is an endless amount of research to prove it. A McKinsey & Company study, for example, showed that companies with more gender diversity on their executive teams were 21 percent more likely to outperform less-diverse teams in terms of profitability. In addition, companies that rank in the top quartile for the ethnic and cultural diversity of executives were 33 percent more likely to be more profitable than those that ranked lower.

A survey of more than twenty thousand publicly traded companies in ninety-one countries by the Peterson Institute for International Economics found that companies with more women holding executive positions in corporate management correlated with increased profitability. In fact, firms with women holding at least 30 percent of top executive positions were shown to add one percentage point of net margin gain compared to those with men-only executive teams.

Back in 2015, I knew we still had a long way to go on this issue, but I was utterly convinced that Salesforce belonged to the tiny minority of tech companies that truly valued gender equality. So I simply did not believe that pay disparities could be pervasive. "Impossible," I told them. "That's not right. That's not how we operate."

Cindy leveled her gaze. Then, in the measured tone she'd used to talk me out of wrongheaded positions in the past, she explained that she'd invited Leyla to join her at this meeting because they had both independently arrived at the same concern. "We surged, we got bigger jobs, we got promoted, and that's when we started to put our heads together," Cindy explained.

Leyla, who's also known for her directness, jumped in. "Look, Marc," she said. "Men at my level are buying expensive Teslas. Maybe it's just a feeling that men make more than women. But maybe it's an ugly fact."

I knew she wasn't implying that any pay disparities were deliberate. Unequal pay is a stubborn, slippery problem in business, and Cindy had brought studies showing that in 2014, a woman working full time earned, on average, about 79 percent of what a man did, according to the U.S. Department of Labor. The Institute for Women's Policy Research had recently found that from 2001 to 2015, women earned roughly half of what men did, even when taking into account time off for family or child care. And, as I later learned, the wage gap persists even for highly educated executives: Data from a 2018 *Financial Times* ranking of the best global MBA programs showed that women earned, on average, 9 percent less than men before receiving their degrees and 14 percent less three years after graduation.

That's all absolutely true, I told Cindy, but how could this issue persist inside a company that works so hard to avoid it?

Cindy sat back in her chair and patiently launched into an explanation of how pay gaps sneak into the workforce. Unconscious bias plays a significant role in how men and women are treated when salaries are set. Women workers often sacrifice better wages for flexible hours, typically because of family considerations (a burden that tends to fall more heavily on women than men). Many, she reminded me, spend years trying to catch up after failing to negotiate aggressively for higher pay early in their careers.

"We can either lead on pay equality or we can follow," Cindy concluded. "But this issue will only get bigger. It won't go away." She added, "We're not a company that follows."

Cindy and Leyla hadn't come to my house just to rattle my cage. They had a proposal. Why not order an audit to conclusively determine whether men and women were being paid equally? Convinced that the data would be vindicating, I immediately agreed to commission a salary review for all seventeen thousand Salesforce employees we had at the time.

"Let's go from top to bottom," I said, "one person at a time."

For a brief moment, Cindy looked relieved. Then I saw a flicker of worry creep back onto her face. Before we went ahead, she told me, she wanted to make sure this audit wouldn't be a hollow exercise. What can't happen, she said, "is we do the assessment, look under the hood, see a big dollar sign, and shut the hood." In other words, she wanted me to commit to *acting* on the results, no matter the price tag; did she have my word that if a wage gap was found, we would close it, immediately?

"Of course I agree," I said.

"Well, you know what it's gonna cost you, don't you?"

Upon hearing this, I'll admit I started thinking like the CEO of a publicly traded company. *What if they're right?* I wondered. *Could it be a $10 million hit? Or $50 million?*

"What's it gonna cost me?" I asked.

"Well, I don't know," Cindy replied.

I had always thought I was more progressive on gender equality than most male technology executives. Now I was about to get the chance to prove it.

"Okay, I agree." I said. "Let's do this."

Data vs. Megaphones

In Chapter Two, I talked about how I'd taken a very public stand against LGBTQ discrimination in Indiana, and later, I would fight a similarly odious bill in Georgia and also North Carolina that required transgender people to use public bathrooms based on their birth sex. I'd always sort of lumped all issues of "equality" in the same basket. But in talking to Cindy and Leyla, I was beginning to realize that gender discrimination is a different kind of monster. The wage gap isn't the result of some bill that got pushed through Congress. Equal pay isn't something most politicians talk about at rallies to fire up their base. There's no one single enemy to identify and go head to head with, nor is there a simple, universal solution to champion.

Instead, it's a pernicious and far-reaching problem that unfolds quietly, everywhere, all the time, behind the closed doors of conference rooms where decisions get made (usually by men). Which is why fighting for gender equality would demand much more than the blunt tools that had worked in Indiana. Rather than simply using my voice, and then employing Twitter as a megaphone to amplify it, this battle would require digging through data, listening to people, asking uncomfortable questions, and examining unconscious behaviors. Anything less would be like trying to perform brain surgery with a butter knife instead of a scalpel.

In late April, as the audit was just getting under way, I decided, in the interest of transparency, to send an all-employee email. "I have been working with Cindy Robbins, Leyla Seka, and the rest of my leadership team to ensure that men and women at Salesforce are receiving equal opportunity and equal pay," I wrote. "This is a multi-year project we are embarking on, but it is an important endeavor for both our company and our industry at large."

At this point, I still believed that the next all-employee email I would send on this matter would be a triumphant one, declaring that we had determined conclusively that across the board, male and female employees of Salesforce were being paid equal salaries for equal work.

Unfortunately, this did not come to pass.

Meanwhile, we assembled a cross-functional team for the pay assessment, and developed a methodology with outside experts that analyzed the entire employee population based on objective factors that determine pay such as job function, level, and location. The assessment grouped employees in comparable roles and analyzed compensation of those groups to determine whether there were unexplained differences in pay among gender globally.

When the results came back a few months later, they left no doubt about one thing. Salesforce *did* have a pay gap. Moreover, it wasn't just an isolated phenomenon in a handful of offices. Glaring differences were scattered throughout the whole company in every division, department, and geographical region. The virus, in other words, was everywhere.

I couldn't help but hang my head. I was disappointed and, frankly, chastened. These problems were so close to home that I'd failed to see them clearly, even as they were unfolding right under my nose. That day, I informed my board and executive team that Salesforce would soon be incurring some additional expenses, as I had every intention of making good on my promise to Cindy.

In all, we found that 6 percent of employees, mostly women but also some men, would need their salaries adjusted. We didn't want to reduce anyone's pay, so we adjusted salaries upward. All told, the total cost of making these adjustments for our U.S. employees worked out to about $3 million: lower than I had feared. That's not a small sum, but given how profoundly appropriate and necessary this was, it seemed like a relative bargain.

In the months that followed, I began to speak out about pay equality—everywhere from a dinner at the Los Angeles home of actress Patricia Arquette, to an innovation summit in Tokyo, to the White House. So you can imagine my astonishment and, to be honest, embarrassment, when Cindy came to see me again.

One year after conducting our first audit and making that $3 million correction, we'd run the numbers again. Turned out we needed to spend *another* $3 million adjusting the salaries of employees whose compensation had fallen out of whack since the last audit. "How can this be?" I asked Cindy and the executive team.

It gave me some relief to discover that these figures were largely a consequence of growth. We'd recently gotten about 17 percent bigger after buying two dozen companies, and it turned out that in the process we hadn't just inherited their technology, but their pay practices and culture, too. As a result, the share of employees who were being undercompensated based on sex, as well as race and ethnicity, had actually increased to 11 percent from 6 percent the year before.

Realizing that this had the potential to become a recurring problem, we decided to take more stringent measures. We devised a new set of job codes and standards and applied them to each newly integrated company to make sure everyone performing similar work was similarly compensated from day one. From there, Cindy's team began reviewing merit increases, bonuses, stock grants, and promotions to root out disparities there, too.

It took some tinkering to get these policies right, but they eventually became part of the Salesforce firmament. In 2018, Cindy and I were interviewed about our gender pay initiative by Lesley Stahl for a segment on *60 Minutes*—a segment that I hoped would encourage other CEOs to take a look at the pay practices at their own companies. We also talked about the reality that, as with most things in business today, equality is a moving target, and we were well aware that our work was far from finished.

Case in point was a customer call I made with our financial-services sales team to JPMorgan Chase in early 2018. I typically wouldn't have gone to this meeting, but I was attending a dinner there that night hosted by JPM's CEO Jamie Dimon, so I decided to tag along. I walked over to the meeting—a brisk fifteen-minute stroll from our Salesforce Tower New York in Bryant Park to the JPM headquarters in midtown—with the team leader, Steve Moroski. Over a quick snack of falafel purchased from a hot-dog stand outside JPMorgan's Park Avenue high-rise, Steve pitched me on his idea to bring Salesforce technology into the Chase consumer-banking network. The pitch was excellent, and I felt good about his plan.

But once we were seated around the long mahogany conference table, my enthusiasm quickly turned to alarm—and disappointment. The sales people Salesforce had sent to make the presentation were all men. Immediately after the meeting I slipped Steve a tersely worded note: "Why do you not have any women sales people?" Then I headed into my dinner.

After receiving what he later called my "love note" to him, Steve immediately told his rapidly expanding team that there were going to be some changes in how they chose its future members: "We hire the best candidate and *she's* out there." I've since noticed Steve often has women account managers lead our sales presentations at the big banks and securities firms. Looking at the *data*, my favorite gauge, I learned that his enterprise banking team of sixty-five sales people had gone from just 16 percent women to 37 percent women. Now one-third of his leaders were women, up from zero.

His comment to his team reflects an important point about our approach to equality. I don't believe we should be hiring any woman who applies simply for the sake of meeting a quota. But I do insist we go the extra mile to find those highly qualified women candidates who we believe would be the best fit for the role, and strive to take unconscious bias out of the hiring process.

Equalizing pay wasn't an easy process, or a cheap one: after our third pay assessment, we'd spent a total of $8.7 million addressing differences in pay based on gender, race, and ethnicity. It has already begun to pay off in incalculable ways, and its benefits will continue to accrue for years. Already, our commitment to equality has helped land us the number one spot on *Fortune's* list of best companies to work for, as well as the top spot on *People* magazine's list of "Companies That Care" two years in a row. And it's contributed to our ability to attract the very best and brightest talent in the country, particularly the enormous amounts of female talent that many of our competitors are failing to tap. For example, Steve Moroski shared with me that once his banking team reached the point where it employed 20 percent women, their hiring of female sales people took off. "We were plugged into a new network, and women wanted to come to Salesforce," he explained.

What all of this has shown me is that inclusion isn't monolithic. The fight for equality is a collection of many battles on different fronts, each one presenting unique challenges and requiring unique remedies. The levers that work to attack one problem may be useless in addressing another. To navigate this, everyone inside a company has to be able to recognize their blind spots and be flexible enough to try new solutions.

Unfinished Business

In early 2018, I noticed a few women around the office, and a couple of men, reading Emily Chang's *Brotopia: Breaking Up the Boys' Club of Silicon Valley*. This account, which *The New York Times Book Review* called "a well-researched history of how Silicon Valley became a glorified frat house," helped me understand that the problem of sexual harassment went far beyond office romances and hot-tub parties. It was a symptom, albeit a serious one, of a much larger and more systemic problem: namely, an organizational culture that was willing to tolerate it.

Since Cindy and Leyla walked into my office in 2015, I've learned a great deal about how a company's culture can breed inequality in ways small and large. "Unconscious bias" is a big one, and unfortunately it's also a swamp you can step into even when your intentions are good. And step into it I still sometimes do.

During a March 2017 event at Salesforce headquarters, I hosted a session to introduce our new product roadmap. The audience consisted of reporters, analysts, and customers, with thousands of others watching via livestream. We were also celebrating Salesforce's eighteenth birthday, so my wife, Lynne, came along.

There were to be four speakers, all Salesforce executives. The first three were men, and when I called each one individually to the stage, I shook their hands and thanked them. When the fourth speaker, a woman, came to deliver her remarks, however, I gave her a quick hug.

After the presentation, Lynne pulled me aside. "You didn't hug the men, so why hug the woman?" she said. "That diminished her; they are *all* professionals."

She was right, of course. I had treated my female executive differently, and until that moment I had zero awareness of it.

I was learning that unconscious bias shows up in all kinds of ways, especially in industries like tech that have historically been largely male-dominated. Ellen Kullman, the former CEO of DuPont and co-chair of Paradigm for Parity, an organization of high-powered business leaders whose goal is to achieve full gender parity in the workplace by 2030, once pointed out something that's both encouraging and, to me, rather daunting. Since men hold the majority of leadership roles in the corporate world, she said, they play a critical role in advocating for women and mentoring them. "Until you level that playing field," Ellen says, "you're going to get that same outcome."

Mentorship is something I've always been comfortable with, and I eagerly encouraged Cindy to pilot a mentoring program targeting high-potential women at the company. When the feedback came back, the reaction was unexpected. While the women appreciated the investment being made, they didn't want to be in a program just for women. It made them feel singled out (not in a good way), as if they were in a cohort that needed to be "fixed." They had a point. These rising stars wanted to be part of a mentoring group for high-potential *employees*—men and women. So we made those adjustments and today have "co-ed" programs in place in both our tech and sales departments.

These missteps have taught me that I have to be more conscious of how I interact with women employees, even when I'm trying to be helpful and more inclusive. Because I'm a man who came up in a male-dominated business, I'm vulnerable to many of the subtle perceptions and expectations that men apply only to women and, to some extent, that women project on men in positions of authority.

Recognizing that I was likely not alone in this, I decided we needed to take measures to proactively address unconscious bias and provide all employees—including top leadership—with the tools needed to drive inclusion in the workforce. So in 2016, we launched a workshop called Cultivating Equality, available at our offices around the world, as well as a Trailhead online learning course on unconscious bias, which was simultaneously open to the general public. We also introduced inclusive hiring procedures aimed at ensuring that our candidate pool reflects our communities to remove bias from the hiring process.

In the end, the most important thing leaders can do to promote equality is to open themselves up, take an honest inventory, listen to people, and never be too proud or defensive to make corrections. There are three mistakes to avoid. First, never convince yourself that you know everything. Second, never refuse to search for the truth. And third, never conclude (no matter how hard you've worked) that the job is finished.

I've learned something else about equality, too. There's often a strong correlation between your ability to make progress and your willingness to ask others for help.

Shepherds Do Not Beget Sheep

On July 5, 2016, Alton Sterling, an unarmed thirty-seven-year-old black man, was fatally shot at close range by two white police officers in Baton Rouge, Louisiana. The following day, another black man, thirty-two-year-old Philando Castile, was pulled over in Falcon Heights, Minnesota, and shot and killed in front of his girlfriend and four-year-old daughter by a white police officer. Unfortunately, neither of these tragic incidents was the first time that an innocent black man had been killed at the hands of a white police officer, and they wouldn't be the last. The two crimes (for which one of the officers would be acquitted and the other never charged) occurring in the span of under forty-eight hours, and the widespread outrage, peaceful demonstrations, and violent protests they ignited, put the issue of racial injustice in America at top of mind.

Later that week, our headquarters lobby screens shared a message of peace in the form of two quotes from Dr. Martin Luther King, Jr., and we sent an email reminding employees that support services were available. I was glad we did those things, but I knew they weren't nearly enough.

On July 9, a photo of Black Lives Matter activist DeRay Mckesson on his knees being arrested during a protest in Baton Rouge went viral on social media. He wore a T-shirt that said #STAYWOKE, with a black version of the Twitter bird logo on the front. I'd always admired Twitter's employee resource group for African American employees, which they call Black Birds (the company's equivalent of our company's BOLDforce). So the next day I tweeted. "Yes that is a @Twitter @Blackbirds logo," I wrote. "Amazing to see tech as a vehicle for social change. Respect."

It took me about fifteen seconds to realize I'd made a huge mistake. Replies poured in, slamming me for hypocrisy and worse. The general view was that someone like me, a CEO in an industry plagued by a terrible record of hiring black employees, had no right to wrap himself around a movement aimed at combating racism.

And my comment touting tech as a vehicle for social change, as many people rightly pointed out, was completely tone-deaf in that moment.

One especially devastating comment contained only three statistics:

Facebook 2% Black
Twitter 2% Black
Salesforce 2% Black

The criticism was absolutely fair. Black employees made up just over 2 percent of our workforce in the United States, and fewer than 4 percent were Hispanic or Latinx. That's not nearly representative of the communities where we live and work.

"That anyone could see a picture of a black man being arrested for protesting against the wrongful killing of another black man and respond 'Hey look at the Twitter logo,' would be mind-boggling if it happened anywhere else. In the tech industry though, it's par for the course," Erica Joy Baker, then a senior engineer at Slack and a founding member of Project Include, told the *Guardian*.

This experience was gutting. I apologized individually to nearly every person who commented on the post, but I was seriously rattled. How could I have thought, even for a second, that this was a reasonable way to show support for racial justice? I'd made the mistake of picking up a megaphone to champion a cause, when I should have been focusing on getting my own house in order.

In that humbling moment, I knew it was a sign. It was clear we needed to make huge changes when it came to racial equality and inclusion at Salesforce. But I had no idea where to start. So I reached out to Molly Ford, a frank and trusted member of our public-relations team. "What is your experience as a black woman working at Salesforce?" I asked her.

She told me it was lonely. There were so few people of color and even fewer leaders of color to serve as role models. She also said she didn't believe there was enough effort being made at Salesforce to help others understand the struggles of underrepresented minorities. Molly quoted an old saying to me: "Shepherds do not beget sheep. Sheep beget sheep," meaning if we were serious about becoming a welcoming place, we had to bring more racial diversity into our ranks, and we needed to give our employees from underrepresented groups a better way to broach issues that impacted them. We'd have to start all over by looking in the mirror *again*. To do this, I needed help. I asked Molly to take a leave from her day job to help me work on this issue, and she agreed.

At our annual midyear meeting for Salesforce's executive leadership in Hawaii, we held a panel on culture. One manager asked how serious the company was about achieving diversity. This time, I didn't wait for someone else to answer. "Equality will be our priority going forward," I said decisively. "Equality is now a core value."

I was committed to do whatever it took to uphold it. That meant accelerating our efforts to promote gender equality, LGBTQ equality, racial equality, and equal pay. Given the long road that stretched ahead, I decided it was time to hire someone to lead all of the company's equality initiatives. I remembered my friend Tony Prophet, whom I got to know when he was a senior executive at Hewlett Packard in the Bay Area. He had since moved to Microsoft as a marketing executive, where he'd launched BlackLight at Microsoft, the company's black-empowerment platform.

Impressed with his work on equality issues, as well as his tech background, we offered him a new position at Salesforce as Chief Equality Officer. It was important that Tony would report directly to me, and that his new department would get all the resources and support needed to champion and advocate for equality within the company and among our stakeholders.

Over the last several years we've established partnerships with workforce development and education organizations such as College Track, which is dedicated to helping students from underserved communities graduate from college. And we partner with college campus organizations and nonprofits like Management Leadership for Tomorrow (MLT), which provides African Americans, Latinxs, and Native Americans with the skills, coaching, and connections to succeed in the world of work.

We've also committed to help close the opportunity divide, giving young people facing barriers to success a path to meaningful careers by donating funds and employee time to underserved local schools and working with organizations such as Code.org, CoderDojo, Hidden Genius Project, and Mission Bit to expand access and participation in computer science in schools. We work with PepUp Tech, a nonprofit built by a group of Salesforce trailblazers that provides underserved students access, skills, and mentorship to begin careers in tech. We have also partnered with organizations, such as Year Up, that provide young adults with high-demand vocational job skills, experience, and support. Our Futureforce global recruiting program, which we introduced in 2014, is focused on attracting a diverse pool of university graduates and urban youth, as well as veterans and their spouses, to Salesforce. Over the past year, 43 percent of Futureforce's new hires in the United States were women or underrepresented minorities.

Our ultimate mission when it comes to equality at Salesforce sounds deceptively simple: for our offices all over the world to look like the larger populations they serve. I'm not just laying this off on our human resources department, however. The Office of Equality provides every senior executive at the company with a monthly tally of the employees they've hired, fired, or lost to attrition and how many of them are women or members of underrepresented minority groups.

As I said, the data is out there and it doesn't lie. We continue to lean into it, and every year we are looking at new slices in order to spot areas where diversity is lacking, expose—and close—pay gaps, and surface problems around hiring, promotion, and retention. The results dictate our strategy going forward.

That Black Birds tweet I'd sent was so profoundly insensitive that I'd deleted it. In a backwards way, though, I was grateful for the backlash it created. It reminded me how important it is for leaders to align their words and behavior. You can make all the empathetic statements you want, but until you figure out how to open doors for people of color and build a welcoming environment for them, you'll never create lasting change. We have miles to go, but I know we will never stop working to make our culture more compassionate, creative, and diverse.

———

At the 2018 World Economic Forum, my co-CEO Keith Block met with Carolyn Tastad, Procter & Gamble's group president for North America. A trailblazer if there ever was one, Carolyn is a fierce advocate for women in business, and Keith left their meeting armed with a better understanding of the issues holding women back in the workplace, on display at P&G's special Davos exhibit. In return, Keith invited her to visit Salesforce's headquarters in San Francisco.

Carolyn's chief focus at the time was reigniting revenue growth in the consumer giant's $30 billion North America business, and naturally, we wanted to be the ones to help her do it. Keith tapped Salesforce's Eric Eyken-Sluyters, our senior executive for retail and consumer packaged goods, to come up with an innovative solution that could help P&G sell more through its channels—everywhere from Walmart to neighborhood convenience stores. When Keith met with Eric and his team the night before the big meeting with Carolyn, however, Keith discovered a serious problem.

There were once again no women on the sales team.

"Eric, seriously?" Keith recalls asking. That's when Eric broke the unfortunate news that the women on Eric's team who were slated to participate had experienced flight delays to San Francisco.

Before P&G and Salesforce executives gathered the next day, Keith asked our head of trailblazer marketing, Cristina Jones, to join the meeting. His goal wasn't to change the gender ratio simply for the sake of appearances, but to bring in a smart, experienced female voice who could add value to the meeting with the P&G president.

Eric made a compelling pitch for how we could leverage data to improve in-store retail execution. But Keith knew we weren't going to win Carolyn's business by sticking to the practical matters at hand. We also needed to show that our companies were aligned around values. He began telling her about Salesforce's values-based culture, then threw it to Cristina to describe the Salesforce trailblazer community and the efforts we'd undertaken to prioritize equality inside our own company. By the time the presentation wrapped up, it was clear to everyone in the room that the discussion had made an impression on Carolyn. "Our brand was elevated in her eyes," Eric told me later.

Shortly thereafter, P&G signed up with us for a major data-analytics project. It was, once again, a valuable piece of business obtained largely, if not primarily, by the force of our four core values.

In Part I, I described the events that forced me to step back and think more deeply about my company and the broader future of business. In the space of a few eventful years, I faced a series of challenges I'd never anticipated. Navigating them taught me some transformative lessons that upended much of what I thought I knew about why Salesforce was a successful business, and how I should lead it. First, the culture we'd built, and the core values underpinning it, are not ancillary to our success over the past two decades. They are in fact the mighty engine under the hood, powering everything. And when I opened that hood, it became clear that our four core values not only created value in their own different ways, they were also intertwined. They worked together to create the momentum that keeps our flywheel spinning.

Building trust, for example, requires creating a culture that always puts the customer first, and making choices that improve the state of the world, not just the bottom line. It requires hiring people who genuinely care about their colleagues, customers, and the broader community, and that's best accomplished by a workforce that is diverse, inclusive, and equal. That's the kind of base you need to stand up for the rights of people both inside the company and across the planet we inhabit.

We also know now that to attract and retain women and minorities in the company, equality needs to be embedded not only in our stated values but in our actions: in our hiring practices, in our retention practices, in how we promote employees up the chain and eventually into leadership roles. Put simply, people want to work at companies where they can trust their employer: to create a safe place for them to work, to pay them fairly, and to give them the same opportunities to advance as everyone else, regardless of gender, race, skin color, or anything else. If these aren't your company's priorities, why would women—or anyone—want to work there?

The bottom line is that building a diverse workforce makes good business sense. Success in the rapidly changing digital age requires an ecosystem that supports continuous innovation. And that demands diversity in every sense of the word. Can you imagine trying to drive innovation and transformation inside your company when everyone looks and thinks the same? That doesn't produce the creative solutions we need to help our customers be successful.

Whether you run a company, lead a small team, or aren't in a management or leadership role yet but aspire to be, success will require you to widen your field of vision to the world while also narrowing it to the organization around you. There's no map for the frontier you are entering. You have to seek out those who can help you blaze that trail into the unfamiliar terrain.

Here's the thing about values: You have to use words to identify them, but they won't create true value for you unless they turn into consistent behaviors. Making values a bedrock of your culture is far more wise and sustainable than applying them selectively or intermittently, or scrambling to put them in place in reaction to a crisis.

All of this might sound like a minefield, but I firmly believe that in the future, equality will be the key to unlocking a company's full and sustainable value. That doesn't mean it's easy to achieve. But those who fail to try will be on the wrong side of history.

PART II

BUSINESS IS THE GREATEST PLATFORM FOR CHANGE

SHARED KNOWLEDGE

Whenever I venture out in public, which is pretty often, I rarely think of myself as the Salesforce CEO. Truth be told, I feel more like the CAQ.

Chief Answerer of Questions.

When you make it known publicly that you intend to create a different kind of business—in our case a business that's equally committed to doing well and doing good—people are going to be curious. They want to know how you operate, what keeps you awake at night, and how well it's all going. You'll be cornered at parties, conferences, charity events, and, in my case, even halftime breaks at Golden State Warriors games.

For nearly two decades, the nature of these questions has evolved dramatically. People who admired our business model wanted to emulate it. Others came from folks who could barely mask their skepticism and were clearly probing for signs of weakness. As Salesforce gained market traction and more public notice, we were asked about practical things, like how we innovate, recruit talent, or decide which charities to support. Lately, however, one question in particular has started elbowing the others aside:

"Tell me about your *culture*."

That word, "culture," has become the hottest term in the corporate lexicon, not just in the United States but all over the world. Yet the way it's often used has always seemed problematic to me. Some business leaders seem to consign it to a glossy brochure under a photo of a carefully curated group of smiling people gathered in a well-appointed office. Others seem to think they've developed a culture by providing gourmet meals and installing Ping-Pong tables.

The truth is that culture is about so much more than just perks and freebies. Culture, at its core, is about how you define and express your values.

Increasingly, people want to work at companies that share their values. Millennial employees, who now make up more than half of our workforce, are teaching us what they believe about the future of work. Younger generations of employees want their work to have a higher purpose. They want to make sure their company is committed to improving the state of the world. If business leaders think it's hard to navigate this now, just wait until the next generational wave enters the workforce. I believe they'll be two or three times more mission-driven.

As companies meet this employee demand, they're realizing this culture needs to be authentic. There's no longer a generic, off-the-rack set of principles anyone can adopt to underpin a culture. It needs to be as distinct as a fingerprint.

From the start of Salesforce, our culture totems have been

surprisingly basic. The main one is a commitment to getting involved in a world beyond our walls. Our people want to help communities; they want a balanced life; they want to help others grow; and they want to make our customers and company successful.

Yet from our determination to build a pioneering software business that runs in the cloud to our decision in 2018 to throw our weight behind a ballot referendum to address the pressing issue of homelessness in San Francisco, we've often found ourselves standing on an island.

Some people roll their eyes at us. They assume we're just virtue-signaling, trying to call attention to ourselves. Others remark that we wouldn't be nearly so bold if we hadn't been posting record quarterly revenue. From the inside, however, those skeptical views do not influence the way we think.

To get big and stay that way for a long time, you don't need an exotic collection of values, you just need good ones. And you can't fake them. If a culture is phony, derivative, halfhearted, or misguided, it will eventually sink you. A genuine culture built on fundamentals like trust and aimed at the goal of business for good is more than enough, but only if it genuinely outweighs the traditional business motives of driving revenue, growth, and profit.

Back when we started Salesforce, few companies were preoccupied with culture. Not only were we early to the party, we've had a twenty-year head start to engage in a process of trial and error.

In Part I, I showed you how difficult and messy, but completely gratifying, that journey has been, but I also tried to give you a glimpse of how that culture you may have imagined at the start becomes a living, breathing, evolving organism. And how, as a leader, it's up to you to evolve along with it. Picking values to live by is the easy part; putting them into practice requires extraordinary attentiveness and persistence.

The management authority Peter Drucker once laid out a simple rule that has always stuck with me: "Culture eats strategy for breakfast." Based on my experience at Salesforce, culture eats *everything*.

All of the business tactics we've deployed, every line of code we've written, and every marketing campaign we've dreamed up over the years are, in the end, ephemeral. Each one could be discarded and replaced at any moment as the world around us changes. It's our culture's ability to evolve with the pace of change, to live and breathe on its own, to be both familiar and dynamic, that really drives us forward. For businesses that want to have any hope of thriving in the future, culture—and the values that define it—is what will drive financial success.

Today's world is so rife with challenging economic, social, and political issues that it's no longer feasible for a company to turn away and conduct business as usual. The bigger you get and the more people you impact, the harder it becomes to simply let your products define you. Over time, your employees and customers, not to mention investors, partners, host communities, and other stakeholders, will want to know your philosophy for doing business. They want to know if you have a *soul*.

We've seen moments when two or more of our values have painfully and publicly come into conflict, but we're getting used to it. Inevitably, these periods of discomfort will come. If your culture is strong, you will survive them. In fact, they may even make you stronger. To us, these situations have always proven to be oddly reassuring. They remind us who we really are.

In the old world of business, proprietary knowledge was a weapon. Sharing your deepest insights was counterproductive because it could only make your rivals stronger. CEOs responded to probing questions with practiced vagueness. I suppose I could have kept these lessons to myself, but that never occurred to me. I can't imagine operating in an environment of trust and transparency at work while simultaneously building soundproof walls to keep the world out.

If Salesforce has taught me anything, it's the power of creating a community that will grow itself by opening its arms to anyone and sharing our values. Everyone at our company believes they have a greater responsibility, and a voice, and the tools at their disposal to be a trailblazer.

In other words, knowledge isn't truly powerful until it's shared.

So as the Salesforce CAQ, I'm always going to answer your questions. I'll tell you what I think the business of the future looks like and give you some prescriptive advice for building your own. That's the purpose of Part II: I want to take you on a journey to see how our trailblazing culture works from the inside out.

SEVEN

OHANA

Redefining Corporate Culture

I'd always been disruptive and entrepreneurially-minded; I'm pretty convinced it's just how I'm wired. The truth is that the instinct to launch a company, and to make excellent products, turn profits, grow and innovate, exists inside millions of us. It's a perfectly natural human endeavor. Here's the problem: When it comes to defining a culture, these entrepreneurial impulses can be a lousy guide. And they depend to a large extent on external forces, such as the economy, competition, and the talent pool, that you can't fully control. If you use those priorities as a guide, you're going to make mistakes, just as I did in the early days.

What you actually need as your guide is a set of principles defining why and how you want to build the company you have in mind. After all, a company is fundamentally made up of people, not things, joined together on a shared mission. And how you approach that mission is a direct by-product of the culture you create.

Dov Seidman, one of the wisest people I know on the subject of business and morality and author of *How: Why HOW We Do Anything Means Everything*, likes to say that culture is something that "grows out of the unique way people at an organization relate to one another, organize their efforts, and govern themselves."

He's right, of course. A company's culture is not just about the people on its payroll, or the customers it works with. Its sphere of influence has to include every single person it touches, even tangentially, including people who may be far enough removed that reaching them isn't even part of your original plan. In the end, defining that culture isn't a matter of drawing a circle of trust around just your employees and customers, it's about widening that circle as much as possible.

To give a few examples: Before Indiana's legislature passed that discriminatory law, I never expected to be in a situation that would require us to take stands on social issues. Until we conducted that salary audit, I had no idea that the issue of unequal pay was something we would have to address. And it wasn't until 2018, when some of our employees complained that our software was being used by Customs and Border Protection at a time when federal agencies were separating migrant children from their families at the U.S.-Mexico border, that we realized that our commitment to doing good would have to extend to examining the way our products were being used. But in each case, our values showed us the way forward.

What I've just said might give you the idea that culture is simply a tool you can use to navigate complex issues. But it's not that simple. Values aren't like an algorithm you can program to tell you whether to use strategy A or B to address issue C. They require far more careful attention, and more active upkeep.

So to the extent that there is a "secret" to our culture, it's the way in which living our values creates a true sense of belonging. By working hard to build a great company together, and focusing on giving back in our communities together, we've built bonds that have grown stronger over time. And the two most important building blocks have been our shared commitment to volunteerism and giving back, and our shared mission in service of our customer.

That shared sense of *purpose and meaning* is why Salesforce's culture has come to embody the Hawaiian concept of *Ohana*. It means "family," but it applies to an extended family including those not even related by blood. I first learned about Ohana as a child during family vacations to Hawaii, a place where I always felt happy and peaceful. As an adult, Ohana came to mean any group of people bound by a responsibility for one another, and by their shared values. That was the culture I wanted for Salesforce from the beginning—one that was inclusive of everyone and would underlie everything we do.

Like a growing child, culture needs to be continuously nurtured as the company gets bigger and ages. I consider this to be one of my most important jobs at Salesforce.

In the two decades of our existence, our culture has evolved in ways I hadn't expected. We adopted numerous new practices to help bring our culture to life, animating it in both subtle and obvious ways as we grew from a start-up into a Fortune 500 company. We've had to be attentive every day in nurturing our culture, especially as we have grown so fast. I believe that vigilance about protecting and nurturing our culture is a key reason why we have been ranked on *Fortune*'s "100 Best Companies to Work For" for eleven consecutive years and have been consistently named among the best places to work in cities around the world.

That's not to say this hasn't been without growing pains—every family has moments of friction that can produce painful, heated arguments like the ones we've sometimes experienced at Salesforce. But I always say that trust needs to be the number one priority, and for many of us, the people whom we trust the most are our family members. Of course, we all have been disappointed by families, and I know not every family is the perfect model for the kind of culture we seek to create. But it's the closest analogy I can imagine.

Some chief executives see the notion of treating employees like family as counterproductive to success. Take Netflix CEO Reed Hastings, who has been known to describe his company's culture and management philosophy as being like "a team, not a family." In fact, the infamous Netflix slide deck, which has been viewed hundreds of thousands of times and is cited often by other executives, likens the company to a pro sports team with "stars" at every position—and makes clear that workers demonstrating anything less than "star" performance have no future at the company.

I can understand the logic of wanting star players performing at high levels in every position, and trading or just letting go of players who aren't contributing as much to the team's mission of winning championships. However, I take a different approach, more like the culture developed by Coach Steve Kerr for my beloved Golden State Warriors. Even though he helms a team, Steve believes that having good *people* is more important that just having good basketball players; he understands that players come and go, but the ethos on the court gets passed down from one game and one season to another. The best teams play together like a family who trust one another to have their back.

Admittedly, there's a spiritual element to Ohana. On corporate retreats in Kona, Hawaii, our executive team can occasionally be found standing together in the warm surf, their toes buried in the hot sand, as they join hands for a traditional blessing ceremony before diving into three long days of examining the company in excruciating detail. For us, Ohana is about so much more than just ceremony and rituals. Ohana means treating our forty thousand employees, our nearly one hundred fifty thousand customers, and the millions of others whose lives we touch, the way we would treat our closest relatives.

But this culture doesn't just exist in our offices. No matter where I am, I want to feel it. I want to feel it when I'm just wandering around the offices, when I'm meeting with customers, even when I'm thousands of miles away talking to other CEOs.

For instance, I recently met with David MacLennan, the CEO of Cargill, the nation's largest privately held company, based in Minneapolis. When we walked out of his office, we were surprised to see a dozen people wearing TRAILBLAZER T-shirts and hoodies congregated in the hallway, waiting to ask us for a picture.

"Are these your employees?" David asked me.

"No, they are *your* employees," I told him. "But they use Salesforce technology here, and so they have become part of our family." They are Salesforce trailblazers—the pioneers, innovators, and lifelong learners who inspire us and represent our Ohana.

Ohana has also become an expression of our ethos, especially as we continue to invite more and more newcomers into our already sizable family. We've added eighteen thousand new employees in the last two years, with no end in sight. So we've had to work hard to ensure that we're infusing our culture into everything we do. It has to guide our thinking when we consider taking stands on social issues. It has to be part of how we brainstorm new products. And it needs to inform how we work every day, including everything from the way we onboard new employees, the design of our new workspaces, and our emphasis on giving back, health, mindfulness, and well-being.

Welcome to the Family

On the first day, we welcome new employees to the family, the Ohana.

Day one employees get a Salesforce badge, backpack, and computer, and spend the morning in orientation. We go over who we are, what we do, and the process for logging on to the corporate systems. We talk about our values and volunteering, how the company gives each employee seven days off every year, with full pay, to volunteer with a nonprofit of their choice. In the afternoon, we show them how serious we are by sending them off to do community service. We do this to create a memorable experience with their new colleagues and to show our employees that our values aren't just some abstract, aspirational notion, or worse, merely words on a corporate slide or plaque. We want to give them an idea about how our values are living values, and how giving back is the heart of our culture.

A month later new employees attend Becoming Salesforce, a daylong boot camp, to learn more about our culture, where executives share their experiences at the company, tips on how to thrive in our fast-paced environment, and an overview of our products. There's a campground where people can get familiar with the various employee resource groups, ethics training, and, of course, Salesforce goodies like T-shirts and stickers.

Equally important, though, is having our existing employees welcome their new colleagues into the Ohana. Just as a family prepares for a new addition, Salesforce has an entire system for ensuring new employees feel at home even before they walk in the door. Each new hire is assigned a "trail guide" for guidance, support, and coaching during his or her first ninety days at Salesforce. We also organize lunches and team meetings for the first few weeks with each new employee's co-workers. In fact, the manager picks up the new employee on orientation day for a special lunch out of the office. When you begin to cement those bonds on day one, we find, they quickly grow stronger.

"Camp B-Well"

Having experienced that major burnout at Oracle before my sabbatical, I know firsthand that the health and wellness of our Ohana must be a top priority. I also knew that it is in *everyone's* interest that our employees and their families feel supported to lead healthier lives. When people are healthy, they are more engaged, more productive, and happier, and more likely to stay with the company.

And they treat our customers and one another with more respect, compassion, and gratitude.

Of course, like most corporations, we subsidize fitness club memberships and offer meditation and yoga classes. But as anyone who has ever not gotten around to taking advantage of such benefits at their company knows, simply offering these programs doesn't necessarily mean they are having an impact. So just as we use data to analyze our pay practices, we use data to determine what wellness programs to offer and evaluate their effectiveness. Our HR team regularly reviews employee well-being claims, looking for any issues that may have bubbled up.

As we passed the twenty-five-thousand-employee mark, we saw a distinct rise in behavioral health issues often linked to stress, such as depression, substance abuse, and anxiety. According to data taken from healthcare claims, which was of course anonymized and aggregated, we found that these diagnoses were rising more quickly than other health issues such as cancer and cardiac problems. We were, after all, growing fast in a fast-growing, highly competitive market and industry—increased stress and associated behaviors were a by-product among some of our Ohana.

The data showed us we had to act. Jody Kohner and Stan Dunlap, senior HR executives, consulted with Dr. Kim Peter Norman, professor of psychiatry at UCSF Medical Center in San Francisco, and identified four critical approaches to address the increasing levels of stress and anxiety. The first is Nourish, providing information to help employees establish healthy eating goals. The second, Revive, is about recharging our bodies and minds with resources for sleeping well, taking time off, and unplugging. The third, Move, focuses on physical exercise and activities to maintain a healthy body. And the last approach, Thrive, provides tools for improving mental health, for managing stress and building resiliency to roll with life's punches.

These four pillars became the foundation for a program we called Camp B-Well. Our executive chef, Bill Corbett, recorded short instructional videos that any employee could stream or download to learn how to cook healthful, nutritious meals, and we brought in the food activist and renowned Berkeley-based chef Alice Waters to talk about the benefits of eating locally and organically. We hosted renowned sleep expert Matthew Walker for a discussion on how sleep can improve health, learning, and performance.

We also asked every employee to add a well-being goal to their V2MOM plan, the goal-setting process we use at Salesforce (which you'll learn more about in Chapter Nine). We encourage employees to draw on the support of the Ohana by posting about their goal—and their progress toward it—on their Chatter profiles. For me, it's been so inspiring to see how many people in our Ohana became committed to prioritizing their well-being.

Mindfulness on Every Floor

I have always sought the advice of many kinds of experts to help me become a better leader, and a better bearer of our culture. That's why I've gone to General Powell to help me incorporate philanthropy into the business, and to MC Hammer to help us adapt his successful "street teams" model to build a base of Salesforce evangelists. So naturally, when I needed help instilling mindfulness training more deeply into Salesforce culture, I went to the Vietnamese Zen Buddhist master Thich Nhat Hanh. I've long been practicing meditation under his guidance, and at that time, due to a curious set of circumstances, the world-revered spiritual leader happened to be staying at my house for six months as he recovered from a debilitating stroke, accompanied by an entourage of thirty monks from the Plum Village monastic community in France.

One day, I invited the monks to the Salesforce office. I thought, perhaps naively, that they'd love what we had going on. I was shocked when they told me they didn't like what they saw at all.

When I asked why, they reported, less than approvingly, that every-one was talking all the time, and working all the time. "That's what we do here," I said. "We work."

My explanation didn't mute their disapproval, but they did offer to help introduce mindfulness to our people. One of the monks, Brother Spirit, agreed to lead a seven-hour meditation session. When it "sold out" in record time, that was evidence enough for me—and the monks—that our people wanted more opportunities like it. Clearly, a one-time seven-hour session wasn't going to cut it. We needed to integrate meditation more fully into our day-to-day culture.

At the time, we were investing heavily in real estate to accom-modate our growth, with new offices in our headquarters of San Francisco and entirely new towers in New York and Indianapolis. I asked the monks what I should do to make them better, more mindful places for our employees.

"You should have a whole floor dedicated to silence," they said.

Obviously they did not understand the square footage prices of commercial real estate in these cities. I would have to negotiate with them.

"What about mindfulness areas on every floor?" I countered.

They approved. From now on, in every office, everywhere in the world, we now have, or will soon have, a small mindfulness room on every floor, a quiet zone where employees can retreat to any time they need to press Pause.

Now, I know this may sound very "California," but this is not just some New Age idea. Mindfulness is top of mind everywhere, and its practitioners are reaping the benefits: not just for their health, but also for attention, focus, and in turn their work perfor-mance. As *The New York Times* reported, a new study that "brings scientific thoroughness to mindfulness meditation" conclusively showed that "unlike a placebo, it can change the brains of ordinary people and potentially improve their health." And it's no coinci-dence that of the more than two hundred accomplished performers, executives, and leaders Tim Ferriss interviewed for his book *Tools of Titans: The Tactics, Routines, and Habits of Billionaires, Icons, and World-Class Performers,* he found that more than 80 percent of them practiced mindfulness or meditation—for reasons you'll read more about in Chapter Nine, "A Beginner's Mind."

Leading with Psychological Safety

Last year at our leadership development program, we invited Brené Brown, a research professor at the University of Houston and author of several bestselling books—most recently, *Dare to Lead,* about building a leadership culture of courage, vulnerability, empathy, and connection—to work with fifty of our top senior executives. This resulted in a very honest and at times uncomfortable half day of discussion about what behaviors support our values, as well as what behaviors threaten to sabotage them. One issue that came up was fear of speaking up or being a bearer of bad news. When this kind of fear permeates a company culture, the results can be disastrous. It can corrode the trust that holds up a culture. For a company or team to thrive, you need a diversity of voices and people unafraid to bring their true selves and willing to speak the unvarnished truth.

In fact, studies show that creating a culture of psychological safety—one in which people trust one another and don't fear speaking their minds—results in smarter risk taking and better problem solving.

Given the high importance we place on our innovation ecosystem at Salesforce, this is a huge priority. That's why our Employee Success (HR) team has been working with globally recognized leaders and experts in the field to advise us on how to ensure that we are practicing what we preach. Attributes like tolerance, integrity, and honesty can't be buzzwords; every single person at the company needs to feel safe enough to live them.

This is why in management meetings, we make a point to see that everyone around the table—even the most junior person—feels comfortable expressing themselves. It's why we commissioned a study to understand the impact that an atmosphere of psychological safety can have on team decision making, innovation, and sales results, and plan to launch workshops and development programs to help employees and teams build the kind of trust needed in order for people to feel comfortable speaking up.

We've also found that psychological safety is enhanced when we are being transparent and employees feel like they can play a part in shaping the future of the company. That's why we livestream our management meetings and allow everyone from seasoned Salesforce veterans to new hires to post questions and make comments that executives can view on the big screens.

Moreover, because we're aware that every family, including ours, is far from perfect, twice a year we conduct a detailed employee survey. We ask employees questions about the culture, about whether they feel valued; and we ask them to rate their superiors on qualities like communicating a clear sense of direction, promoting an inclusive work environment, and whether the managers take responsibility versus assign blame. We asked pointed questions about our ethical behavior. The answers are confidential, but we make all the aggregate scores public so teams can review them and identify areas they need to improve. It also provides employees with useful data when they are deciding whether to transfer to a different department.

On our latest survey, we included even more poignant questions, such as whether people felt there was a culture of politicking and backstabbing as ways to get things done or whether they were feeling burned out or bullied. You'll never get direct answers if you don't start by asking the hard questions directly. And you'll never build a trusting culture unless you directly address those types of divisive or debilitating behaviors.

There's nothing more critical to psychological safety than inclusion, which is why we encourage employees to join our Equality Groups, affinity groups that provide a safe space for people to connect around various aspects of their identity, from race and gender identity to sexual orientation to religion. This has become such a central part of our culture that today about half our employees are involved in Equality Groups, up from one in four two years ago.

The beauty of our Equality Groups is how they empower people to speak up for their communities when they need it the most, while also providing a forum to invite allies of different identities. When something happens in the world that impacts our employee community, members set up Equality Circles, which are safe spaces to have healthy, productive, and constructive conversations. In this way employees can feel heard rather than suffering in silence at their desks, and it helps to build awareness and empathy across the company.

For example, in January 2017, when the Trump administration separated families at the U.S. border with Mexico, several employees hosted an Equality Circle. Similarly after white-supremacist demonstrations and violence in Charlottesville, employees gathered to discuss their feelings and fears.

One of our newest Equality Groups, Faithforce, is currently the fastest-growing, with a thousand members in less than a year. Two employees started this group with the support of our Chief Equality Officer, Tony Prophet. He told me how employees were holding secret prayer meetings because they weren't certain that it was allowed, and how a director of content experience, Sue Warnke, had confided to him that she was a born-again Christian but worried that she should tuck her cross necklace inside her blouse at the office.

With more than half of people in the United States saying that faith—whether Muslim, Buddhist, Sikh, Jewish, Christian, Catholic, or anything else—is the core element of their identity, we want *all* employees to feel safe bringing their full authentic selves to work. So as you can imagine, nothing made me prouder than when

Joe Teplow, whose company Rebel we acquired last year, told me about what he called a "remarkable moment of religious harmony powered by Salesforce." He was about to recite a Jewish prayer in one of the mindfulness rooms of our New York tower when Yousef Abbasi, a solutions engineer, walked in to perform his midday Muslim prayer. Joe moved over to make room, and they prayed beside each other in the languages of their religions.

Fun

I still think of Salesforce as a scrappy, trailblazing start-up. It's part of our cultural mindset. True, at the time of this writing more than twenty years into our story, we've risen to the top of the CRM market and occupy beautiful office towers around the world emblazoned with our name. But we haven't lost the youthful enthusiasm and trailblazing spirit that has fueled our growth. In many ways this attitude is expressed simply by not taking ourselves too seriously. Having fun is essential to bringing that part of the company ethos to life.

In fact, fun and play are integral to our culture, and not just because they make Salesforce a more enjoyable place to work, but rather, because they improve *how* we work. Our employees can spend strenuous hours with their noses to the grindstone, trying to meet our goals. Having some levity goes a long way toward reducing tension and restoring focus. It helps in cultivating a beginner's mind. As the Dalai Lama says, "Laughter is good for thinking because when people laugh, it is easier for them to admit new ideas to their minds."

It's why, if you walk into a Salesforce office, you'll see Astro, Codey the Bear, and even a charismatic Einstein, all in bigger-than-life 3D form perfect for taking selfies—not exactly what you'd expect to see when you enter the headquarters of a leading business software company. You'll find these characters adorning our website, business cards, and sales materials, too. I remember that when IBM CEO Ginni Rometty and I reviewed our companies' collaboration, the documents displayed our characters in a national park. At first, this playful scene was clearly off-putting in the world of staid Big Blue. "What are these cartoons?" she puzzled. I explained that our characters represent our products and the national park setting conveys our devotion to family, where many have spent great vacations. Then Ginni lit up, and I could tell she understood. "My happiest memories growing up were family trips to our national parks."

Research on what makes people happy shows it's not things. It's experiences—which is why we host nearly five thousand "official" events a year as well as frequent informal gatherings and dinners in our top cities. It's why I invited the magician David Blaine to a recent dinner in New York City (he ate a wineglass) and why we've had amazing artists such as Yo-Yo Ma, John Legend, Janelle Monáe, Eddie Vedder, and Jewel perform for customers, and amazing artists—most recently Alicia Keys, Red Hot Chili Peppers, Lenny Kravitz, and Metallica—put on concerts at Dreamforce. We want our trailblazers to have unforgettable experiences and share in the fun of our Ohana.

The World's Best Living Room

Culture is more visceral than intellectual, which is why I often find myself asking: "Does this *feel* like Salesforce?"

That question was certainly on my mind when I visited our new Paris office on Avenue Octave Gréard for the first time, in the summer of 2015. It's a striking piece of architecture dating back to 1925 and just one block from the Eiffel Tower. But as soon as I stepped into the entryway I felt that there was something wrong.

In the lobby of this exquisite neoclassical building was a Hawaiian koa wood table. "Why is this here?" I asked. "This seems like such an unusual thing to put here."

"We were told this is what you want," was the response from the team giving me the tour. That's when I thought, *Wow, we're in trouble.* It was a revelation. My reaction wasn't so much about the design choice as the fact that someone had thought that simply outfitting the lobby with a piece of Hawaiian wood could signal our culture! Because we were growing fast and occupied with other problems, I hadn't stopped to think about how the offices where people work every day—our physical spaces—did or didn't reflect our culture.

When I got back to San Francisco I walked up and down each floor of our buildings, which make up our urban campus. With all the incredible growth over the years, our workspaces had been added somewhat piecemeal, the result being, I suddenly realized, that each new addition reflected its own moment in time. We looked like very different companies depending on what door you opened; there was no consistency in the spaces we were creating for our employees and visitors. Worse yet, it also felt much too "corporate." We could be any nondescript company!

Clearly, we were missing a huge opportunity to create a more consistent brand experience and physical environment: a cultural identity that would be conveyed anytime you entered a Salesforce office anywhere in the world. The good news was redesigning our spaces with an entirely new look would be a celebration of our culture *and* an opportunity to unleash the creativity of our team.

I was fortunate to have Elizabeth Pinkham as my guide when I dove headfirst into this massive project. Elizabeth had been responsible for managing Dreamforce since its inception, so she had a rock-solid understanding of how to bring our culture to life at events. Now I was about to have Elizabeth, who was employee number 51 at the company, do the same for our workspaces. At that time, we were working on opening a new thirty-story office building at 350 Mission, which we dubbed Salesforce East. It was the perfect place to pilot the rollout of our new workspace design.

During this process I was struck with two bursts of inspiration. One came from a Zen phrase: "A garden is not complete until everything is taken out of it." The other came from a quote often attributed to Einstein: "Look deep into nature, and then you will understand everything better."

So I called upon my beginner's mind, erasing any preconceived notions, and took my cues from nature. I envisioned a workspace that radiated calm, not exactly a Zen monastery, but bringing the outside world inside the building with natural light, real plants, rocks, warm colors, natural woods, and of course, environmentally sustainable materials. I imagined the floor covered in green grass and with gravel walking paths, like an urban park, and all the desks exposed to the best light and views.

It was easy to paint a vision in my mind, but I soon learned the complexity of making it a reality: choosing the carpets, fabrics, furniture design, wood grains, wallpaper, paint colors, glass, and more. We connected with the creative team at Burberry, a Salesforce customer, to learn about their design philosophy and how their stores are brought to life. They suggested we build a physical mockup or "mock floor" to see how everything would look in life size. So we built conference rooms and tried out different carpet options, furniture, and lighting—evaluating every nuance of the evolving design. The carpet, made of recycled fishnet, evoked grass weaving through gravel paths, and ultimately the feeling of nature became central to the design. Throughout this entire process, I visited the mock floor frequently and offered feedback on how to make the space feel less corporate, more residential, differentiated, connected with nature—in other words, more Salesforce.

The transformation was amazing, but I couldn't shake the feeling that something was still missing. The natural effect was calming, but there wasn't enough color, I remember telling Elizabeth as we toured the office one day. We needed some kind of art.

Then it hit me: Our people!

"We can put up a video screen or a photographic display that shows employees, customers, and community members," she suggested.

"Think bigger," I told her.

That's when our "culture galleries" were born. Nearly life-sized photographs of our Ohana, taken at various events and volunteer activities, were hung on the walls of every floor and elevator lobby. Inspired by a visit to the Museum of Modern Art in San Francisco, Elizabeth showcased the photos in white metal frames. After all, how better to celebrate our people than to elevate them to art?

Nearly everyone who has visited our offices, from Target CEO Brian Cornell and Thrive Global CEO Arianna Huffington to Canadian prime minister Justin Trudeau and reporters from *The New York Times,* has walked in and inevitably said, "Wow. This feels so different!" Whether they realize it or not, what they are feeling is the physical expression of our culture, in all its dimensions. That was my goal—to bring our culture to life.

You feel it the moment you walk into any Salesforce office now. Thanks to that eye-opening Paris visit, I now understand the magic of the large ground-floor lobbies in our buildings where we welcome employees, customers, and the community. In addition to massive screens covering entire lobby walls with changing art, you'll find coffee, snacks, roving greeters outside the security desk, special events, networking opportunities, and even DJs. I want every employee and visitor who walks through our front doors to experience our culture!

But my favorite feature of every new Salesforce tower, from our San Francisco headquarters to New York, Indianapolis, London, Tokyo, and others, is the Ohana floor. Normally, the top floor of a big office tower is reserved for top executives—some companies even make it accessible only by a special, private elevator. Well, I completely rejected that practice, and decided to make the top floor in every tower (and its stunning views) a space that is open to all employees to use for meetings, events, and collaboration during the workday, and invite nonprofits and community groups to enjoy it for free on the weekends.

In 2017, I took an outside construction elevator to the sixty-first floor of the new Salesforce Tower, under construction in downtown San Francisco. Once completed, it would become our new headquarters—as well as the tallest office building west of the Mississippi. The top floor was magical, with stunning views of the Golden Gate Bridge, the Pacific Ocean, and all the major landmarks of our city. Elizabeth and I literally had our heads in the clouds as we stood on the slab of concrete and tilted our faces toward the open sky.

The only question was how to design the floor in a way that would do justice to this fabulous perch.

"Let's create the world's best living room," I told Elizabeth.

The living room in the clouds ended up being a warm and welcoming space with 360-degree views and a coffee bar, comfy furniture, and window seats for hanging out. We covered the beams in thousands of living plants and flowers and even brought in a Steinway piano. Then we hung up a sign that read OHANA FLOOR, ALL ARE WELCOME.

EIGHT

GIVING BACK MEANS LOOKING FORWARD

Investing in the Trailblazers of the Future

On an unusually warm September morning in 2017, I joined several carloads of Salesforce employees for a short convoy over to Visitacion Valley Middle School in San Francisco.

In the several years since Salesforce had "adopted" the school, small contingents from our office had been going there regularly. They dedicated their paid "volunteer days" to everything from mentoring the students on computer science, to backing up the teachers by working with individual students during classes, to just shelving books in the library.

Today was different. The middle-schoolers wanted to turn the tables, and today they would be teaching us. Specifically, they wanted to show us a few new projects our employees had helped them dream up.

The kids demonstrated a "smart" mirror they'd designed that displayed a calendar and a digital readout of the day's news and weather. They showed us a selfie booth built from scratch, and a musical instrument made of blobs of slime that they had wired for sound. Another group led us on a tour of the basketball court, which had just been transformed with a major assist from my co-founder Parker Harris, who had volunteered his time one night and ended up staying until daybreak painting lines on the asphalt.

As our guides at Vis Valley led us from one stop to the next, their pride and enthusiasm for learning were infectious. I remembered what it was like to be that age—to be so thoroughly enchanted by the wonders of programming in particular and possibilities of the world in general. I couldn't help but think about how thoroughly these curious children embodied the trailblazer spirit. They were experiencing life with true beginners' minds, and were eager to bring others along with them on their journey of discovery.

One of the most memorable parts of this visit was witnessing the profound impact of one particular Salesforce volunteer: product innovation manager Kim Chouard. Kim had already made a major impression at Salesforce. He was something of a phenom who had come to his passion for technology and education early; at ten years old he started his own business in building company websites. By the age of twenty-five, he'd gone up against some of our most seasoned engineers and won seven internal hackathons with his own product concepts. And even as he was giving 110 percent at work, he was simultaneously running an after-school coding club he started for underserved students in the Vis Valley library.

Every Thursday, Kim showed up to teach the kids the basics of computer science, programming, and 3-D printing, as well as crucial soft skills like teamwork and problem solving that were critical in the classroom—and that would become even more critical when these young innovators eventually entered the workforce.

On this portion of the tour, one student, Lilian Emelife, proudly demonstrated no fewer than four robots she had built herself. Another student, Carolina Mendiola, used a 3-D printer to create the components for a fully functional remote-controlled robot—then assembled it right in front of us. I might be a veteran of the tech business, but on that day I saw the promise and possibilities of technology through the eyes of a curious child.

During a visit to the playground later that day, one parent of an eighth grader approached Vis Valley's principal with an urgent question. Her son was graduating from the school that year, she explained. "Which high school has the best coding program?" she asked.

Principal Joe Truss stopped in his tracks. In all his years at the school, he'd never been asked that question before. That was because in the past, barely any of these kids had even known what coding was, let alone identified it as something they wanted to do more of. But the exuberance these kids exhibited was astonishing: unlike anything I'd ever witnessed at the many product demos, conferences, and trade shows I'd attended in the years since founding Salesforce. I was floored.

It's natural for a large, growing company with a healthy commitment to building a better world to focus its attention on the weightiest, most urgent global issues. But what this one morning signified to all of us was that while all acts of giving back are paramount, none is more powerful than giving back in the form of learning and knowledge. The time, money, and resources we'd devoted to that school might seem small when compared to the sum of our charitable work, but the dividends are tremendous. Every dollar of your money and every minute of your time that you spend delivering knowledge—and the tools to attain it—to kids and teenagers is an investment in both the trailblazing innovation of the future and in the workforce of tomorrow.

Whether it happens inside or outside the classroom, these investments in education and in learning were the soul of the culture we've built at Salesforce.

Several years ago, we began focusing our philanthropic efforts on building a genuine partnership with our local Bay Area schools because we wanted to help give kids in our community an equal opportunity to a high-quality education. But let me be clear: Our public schools need people to show up and care more than they need the donations of benefactors. They need people who can contribute professional expertise mentoring students, assisting teachers, or even applying a fresh coat of paint. All of those activities are equally powerful tools for change, and Salesforce employees are deploying them all over the world.

This initiative had been born in part out of a visit I had made to one of my neighborhood public schools. Without a plan, or even an appointment, I'd walked through the doors of Presidio Middle School on a fact-finding mission. I knew going in that like many multicultural schools in the Bay Area with students from diverse socioeconomic backgrounds, Presidio was woefully underfunded and understaffed. After dodging my way through the obstacle course of students racing down the hall, I found my way to the principal's office. Once inside, I introduced myself and asked its occupant one question: "How can I help improve this school?"

The principal wasn't sure how to respond. We had never met and he may have thought he was in for an awkward parent discussion. But once he realized what I was really asking—and that I was serious—he promised to get back to me with an answer.

A few weeks later, hundreds of middle school students sat cross-legged in the crumbling asphalt courtyard that passed at that time for the school's playground. I told the kids that I wanted to help make Presidio the "best school in the universe."

This impromptu meeting in the principal's office turned out to be the first of hundreds more of such meetings at public schools all over the world.

Getting Off the Sidelines

Our collaboration with local schools may have begun to blossom after I walked through those doors of Presidio Middle, but really, the seed had been planted long before.

In April 1997, I had just returned to Oracle from my sabbatical in India determined to do more with my life than advance my career in Silicon Valley. My boss, Larry Ellison, asked me to go to Philadelphia to attend the Presidents' Summit for America's Future, chaired by General Powell.

Now here I was, attending an event in Independence Hall, the building where the U.S. Declaration of Independence and Constitution were adopted, surrounded by former presidents, governors, mayors, cabinet members, and many of the nation's top CEOs. To an ambitious thirty-two-year-old looking to expand his impact, it was an awe-inspiring scene.

The Summit's goal was to mobilize America's citizen power in a united effort to solve the problems facing our society—especially those that threaten young people, such as inadequate healthcare, drug abuse, and lack of education needed to compete in the global economy. General Powell wanted us to get involved in what later became a nonprofit called America's Promise, which works to improve the lives of millions of at-risk youth in the nation. It was a pivotal moment.

I couldn't believe that I was hearing the same message from General Powell, one of the most respected public servants, that I had heard from Amma, the hugging saint, during my visit in India. He offered a pledge, which I took, and it would end up influencing me profoundly:

"We pledge to reach out to the most vulnerable members of the American family, our children. They are at risk of growing up unskilled, unlearned or, even worse, unloved. . . . All of us can spare thirty minutes a week or an hour a week. All of us can give an extra dollar. All of us can touch someone who doesn't look like us, who doesn't speak like us, who may not dress like us, but, by God, needs us in their lives."

I had never heard this concept expressed: that business could be about solving social problems. And I'd certainly never heard a more persuasive or urgent call for businesses to focus on giving back by investing in our nation's young people.

"This is about Americans getting off the sidelines and getting onto the playing field," General Powell said in his remarks.

I came back from the event inspired to do just that. I soon met with Larry and convinced him that Oracle should become part of America's Promise. He agreed, and we decided to help in the area we know best: by bringing networked computers to economically disadvantaged schools. In the first year, we placed six thousand computers in schools everywhere from Los Angeles to Israel.

One was MacFarland Middle School, an inner city school with two thousand students in northwest Washington, D.C. We had a plan to install a hundred networked computers, but we had failed to account for the fact that it was the close of the financial quarter, and everyone at Oracle was scrambling to make their sales numbers. As a result, we were short of volunteers. It was over 100 degrees on the day we needed to carry those hundred computers up three flights of stairs, and we didn't have the people to do it. Eventually, the computers got delivered, but so did the message that this cause just wasn't a priority for the team at Oracle.

That was when I began to understand the value of creating an organizational culture where people know that it's important to show up. It was wonderful and generous that Oracle was committing to upgrade computer equipment in schools, but giving back wasn't connected deeply to the culture of the company, so no one felt compelled to exert any extra effort to actually make it happen. I resolved right then—two years before leaving Oracle—that when I eventually had my own company, things would be different.

The 1-1-1 Model

In 2000, about a year after my co-founders and I launched Sales-force, we had some fifty employees, which was enough critical mass to mobilize volunteers and do some good in the world. However, we were a young and fast-growing start-up and didn't have the time or expertise to build up the philanthropic side of things ourselves. We needed to convince someone to come on board and help.

Suzanne DiBianca, a management consultant with a background in technology implementations as well as corporate foundations, turned out to be just the person for the job, but when we first met about the position, I could tell she was skeptical of our intentions. The dot-com boom had created enormous fortunes, both real and on paper (many of which would evaporate in the ensuing dot-com crash). Several of those entrepreneurs were talking about how they would donate portions of their personal wealth to charitable causes, but it was turning out to be mostly that: just talk.

I knew I needed to convince her that Salesforce was committed to doing more than just arbitrarily giving a few dollars to the founders' pet causes. I explained what I had learned from my Oracle experience about the challenges of integrating philanthropy into a corporate environment, and I assured her that we were building a different kind of company. I told her that Salesforce had a mission: We would be dedicated to giving back as much as we were to our core values.

The truth of the matter was that giving back had been baked into every one of our core values from the beginning. After all, the very act of helping others develops and demonstrates trust: It shows employees and customers that we're motivated by more than money. And the way I wanted to give back—by investing in the workforce of tomorrow—is all about ensuring that we will continue driving the kind of trailblazing innovation that will help our customers succeed not only today, but many years into the future. And finally, our focus on improving access to education for all is far and away the best antidote to inequality.

Once Suzanne grasped that this wasn't smoke and mirrors, she accepted the offer to lead our fledgling efforts. Salesforce already had innovative new technology and an innovative new business model; now Suzanne and I were determined to create a new philanthropic model to complement them.

We sought out advice from companies like Ben & Jerry's, which had successfully created a philanthropic foundation with donations of both profits and employee time. We talked to other Silicon Valley start-ups, such as eBay, which had endowed its foundation with $1 million of corporate stock before going public the year before. We learned how Cisco was donating product, as well as employee time, to help nonprofits get connected to the Internet. Alan Hassenfeld, chairman of the toymaker Hasbro (who would later become a Salesforce board member), shared how Hasbro employees were given four hours a month of paid time off for community service. And we learned about how the outdoor apparel company Timberland donated up to forty hours per year of employee time to volunteer through social service agencies around the world.

After a few weeks of reflecting on these examples, it dawned on me that our new model needed to integrate *all* of our resources—our money, products, equity, and people. The answer: Take 1 percent of equity, 1 percent of product, and 1 percent of employees' time and put them into our own nonprofit. This way, rather than pursuing random acts of philanthropy, we would fully embed giving back into our culture. This model would allow us to distribute funding and support on a consistent basis, and we would rigorously track the impact of our efforts.

Coming up with a memorable way to describe our new model of corporate philanthropy was easy—we just went with the simplest formulation: 1-1-1. Getting it up and running was pretty simple, too, since we didn't yet have much by way of resources in any of the categories. We had only a few employees. We had yet to launch a product. And we had zero equity. What we did have, though, was a deep-seated belief in the power of giving, and the energy to back it up. This turned out to be more than enough.

⸻

Since day one, *every* single employee we have hired has received paid days off to volunteer wherever they choose—and we match their donations to whatever cause is most important to them, up to $5,000. My goal was to fuse philanthropy so completely into our culture that it couldn't be disentangled from the core business, and that included making it easy for everyone to give of their time and talents in the ways that work for them.

By June 2000, we were ready to publicly launch the Salesforce Foundation. From the beginning, we knew that if we wanted to truly engage all members of our Ohana in this mission, employees would have to have a strong voice in how we allocated the foundation's funds—and that *they* would have to be the ones to decide what causes to support with their seven days per year of paid volunteer time off (VTO for short). We've found that employees today are more likely to participate in giving back if they have a say in where the money or their volunteer time is going. Suzanne called this the "democratization" of giving back, and as the foundation grew under her guidance, employees took our corporate philanthropy in myriad directions.

Employees volunteer at hospitals, schools, food banks, and other community institutions, locally and as far afield as Cambodia, several African countries, and Tibetan refugee camps in India and Nepal. When massive disasters like Hurricane Katrina hit, employees also volunteer to provide aid on the ground, helping to rebuild areas and get schools back up and running.

When a disaster of great magnitude occurs, there are many urgent priorities. People need medical care, food, water, and shelter. But we were struck by how *access to information, knowledge net-*

works, and data—and the computer literacy to utilize it—would help local aid workers and governments manage those efforts, and do more with less.

So when the 7.0 earthquake devastated Haiti in 2010, affecting 3 million people, for example, Salesforce not only donated to relief funds, including matching employee donations, we also provided Haitian government and local organizations like Sean Penn's J/P Haitian Relief Organization with free Salesforce technology that would allow them to capture data about those being housed in the shelter camps. Then we flew in fifty employee volunteers to install computers at a primary school in an impoverished and densely populated neighborhood in Port-au-Prince. Similarly, when Hurricane Maria devastated Puerto Rico in 2017, employees raised $250,000 to donate to the cause and volunteered on the island to help with the rebuilding.

Our single biggest opportunity for impact, however, is when we have most of our Ohana gathered together. Dreamforce isn't just our biggest customer event, it's our biggest giving-back event of the year. We've collected a million books to donate to schools here and around the world, such as newly constructed schools in Nepal. We joined with Rise Against Hunger (then known as Stop Hunger Now) to package a million meals for communities suffering from limited food resources and poverty. An annual Dreamforce concert raises money for the UCSF Benioff Children's Hospitals ($70 million and counting).

Over the last twenty years, Salesforce has given about $300 million in grants and our employees have volunteered more than 4 million hours in communities around the world. But here's my favorite stat of all: A whopping 88 percent of our employees give back. And as we continue to grow, so will those numbers.

It's not just the recipients of our time and donations who have benefited from these efforts. Giving back has been linked to improved productivity, employee satisfaction, and talent recruitment, according to research from Indiana University's Lilly Family School of Philanthropy. Our own data shows that giving back is the second-highest reason why new hires join Salesforce, and it ranks in the top three reasons why employees stay. Sure, we have gorgeous office buildings outfitted with meditation rooms and barista bars, and it certainly doesn't hurt that we compensate our employees fairly and equally. But the forty thousand people at Salesforce are motivated by more than all that. They care about doing something for others. They want to help local communities. They want to help our children get the best education possible. They want to help bridge the technology divide and prepare the workforce for the shock waves of the future.

Teaching Possibility

In its early days, the Salesforce Foundation was primarily a vehicle for making grants to nonprofits, based on the equity we set aside ahead of the IPO. We gave thousands of nonprofits, NGOs, and educational institutions up to ten free subscriptions to Salesforce technology and provided assistance in using our software to connect with their students, donors, staff, and other stakeholders. As the demand continued to grow and organizations came back for more subscriptions, we made a decision that has amplified our giving exponentially.

We realized we were in a unique position as the philanthropic arm of a company that develops and sells customer relationship management. Every nonprofit (of which there are more than 1.5 million in the United States alone), NGO, and educational institution has "customers"—whether they're donors, students, alumni/ae, staff, partners, or clients. And these organizations need a tool for managing those customer relationships (across sales, customer service, marketing and commerce), just like any other business. By offering them additional subscriptions at a steep discount, we removed a significant barrier—price—to the efficiencies that such a tool could offer. At the same time, even at a discounted price, these subscriptions began bringing in revenue that we could put back into our communities.

These material breakthroughs in the nonprofit world also taught us an important lesson. At the end of the day, Salesforce, like any other technology company, is in the business of helping our customers access, organize, and make sense of information. This is, of course, a function essential to organizations, for-profit and non-profit alike. But developing the ability to tap the power of information, we realized, is also critical for those who will be running and leading those companies and organizations in the future.

Even back when our nascent company had zero products and just a handful of employees, I knew that if we wanted Salesforce to become a trailblazing company, we would need world-class talent. Which meant we needed to invest in those places where future trailblazers could acquire the education and skills they would need to succeed in the digital, information-economy workforce: our schools and youth institutions.

So one of our earliest projects, which we undertook in partnership with General Powell's PowerUP program, was putting computers in after-school centers, including one at the Embarcadero YMCA across the street from our office. We secured space in the Y's windowless basement, where our employees painted the walls with blue skies and white clouds (like parts of Salesforce's offices). Then we installed rows of computers loaded up with the latest technology in place of a bunch of antiquated, useless ones. When the kids came in after school, they were greeted not only with functioning technology, but with "live" help to teach them how to use it—our employee volunteers.

In 2012, we were giving grants and volunteering for all kinds of organizations, including youth organizations, public schools, charities, homeless shelters, and more. On one hand, it felt great to be supporting so many causes we cared about. But on the other, I worried we weren't delivering meaningful impact with this scattered approach. My close friend Ron Conway, a legendary Silicon Valley VC, philanthropist, and Salesforce.org board member, was close to then San Francisco mayor Ed Lee and suggested that we meet to discuss what the city needed most. At my favorite breakfast spot, Ella's, I asked Mayor Lee (who passed away in 2017) what he wanted his legacy to be. He said one word: "Education." After a long pause, he continued: "Especially in middle school, that's where a kid's fate is largely determined. . . . And I would like to give our kids the opportunity, when they graduate, to see themselves working at tech companies like yours."

A few years later, Mayor Lee began working with one of those very kids, Ebony Frelix Beckwith. Ebony, who is now our chief philanthropy officer, grew up in an underserved section of San Francisco (actually a few blocks from Visitacion Valley), and would daydream about someday working in the gleaming towers downtown when she tagged along with her single mother to her secretarial job. After graduating with a degree in computer science, she worked in operations at financial firms and then joined Salesforce as chief of staff in technical business operations. There was no question in my mind that she was the right person to bring a more data-driven approach to the business of giving back at Salesforce.org.

Together with Rob Acker, Salesforce.org's chief operating officer at the time—and now CEO—Ebony and Suzanne pored over the data to see where employees were volunteering and what would be sustainable in the longer term as we sought to prioritize our philanthropic efforts around public school education. Perhaps where we landed was no surprise: We would double down on computer science education, injecting STEM education into all the schools in the district.

A year later, in 2013, San Francisco schools superintendent Richard Carranza (who went on to become chancellor of the New

York City Department of Education) paid me a visit. He wanted to know if we'd be willing to donate a few million dollars to install Wi-Fi in middle schools and buy some classroom laptops. "You guys need to think bigger! What does nirvana look like for the schools?" I asked him. "You just have to tell us what you want."

Eventually, Salesforce pledged $100 million over a decade to the San Francisco Unified and Oakland school districts. But unlike conventional corporate gifts, ours comes with hands-on assistance from our employees, who have volunteered forty thousand hours (thus far) to mentoring students in the classrooms of these two school districts alone.

As a result, San Francisco became the very first school district in the United States to have a computer science curriculum for *every* grade. We have more Wi-Fi in more classrooms, more full-time teachers and coaches for math and technology, and smaller class sizes. And the results are measurable. A full 90 percent of San Francisco's public school students are now proficient in computer science, and we've seen a 2,000 percent increase in girls and 6,600 percent increase in underrepresented groups taking computer science. In my mind, that progress, more than how much money or time we donate, is the real measure of success.

Encouraged by these results, we're doing similar work with school districts where we have offices around the globe. In Indianapolis, for example, the location of our second-biggest hub in the United States, we gave $500,000 to the public school district. With about 90 percent of our employees giving their time in the local schools and nonprofits, they spent sixty-five thousand hours volunteering in Indiana last year alone.

Sometimes, though, the impact of our volunteers on the lives of students and young people isn't just about hours or grades or test scores. Rather, it lies simply in showing them *what's possible.* That's part of the reason why Stephanie Glenn, an early member of our New York hub who has risen from sales manager to vice president, has made volunteering a primary team-building activity. Stephanie and her sales team have taught financial literacy at a school in Queens, and they have brought on interns from Year Up, a workforce development program for young adults without college degrees. Many, like sales intern Britnee Alvarez, end up getting hired by Salesforce for a full-time job.

"You can't be what you can't see," as the saying goes—and we want these kids to see a bright future for themselves, at a company like ours. That's why, in 2018, when Patrick Stokes, an executive based in New York, adopted the Dual Language Middle School, where 86 percent of the students receive free lunch, he did more than set up a coding program. He and Jennifer Stredler, a Salesforce.org vice president, worked with principal Kristina Jelinek to bring 32 students described by the school as "on the cusp" (not the highest performers, but with more potential than they may be demonstrating) to Salesforce Tower in Manhattan.

Patrick and Jenn, and several other Salesforce employees, arranged what they called a "rotating career panel," essentially connecting the middle school students with small groups of employees from various teams, enabling them to ask what we did, how we did it, and, in some cases, what we earned! Whether it was the impact of these inspirational chats or the free Salesforce swag, several left that day with a goal: "I want to work someplace like this after I go to college."

And many of them have. This was the goal of creating Futureforce, a diverse set of programs that includes adopting local public schools to address K-12 STEM education, partnering with nonprofits and NGOs on vocational training, recruiting from universities and community colleges, and creating hundreds of apprenticeships for urban youth, more than half of whom we've hired.

Giving Back by Skilling Up

When we think about educating communities that lack resources, our minds tend to go straight to public school systems. But children and teenagers are no longer the only demographic in need of better access to educational resources. With the rise of AI and robotics, workplaces around the globe are facing a wholesale transformation. For our customers across many industries, routine tasks are increasingly being outsourced to machines. To survive in a world where automation is rendering so many jobs—and even entire careers—obsolete will require an education of a different kind. That's why workforce development has also become a priority for Salesforce.

According to the World Economic Forum's 2018 *The Future of Jobs* report, more than 50 percent of all employees will require significant re-skilling by 2022. People working in sales and manufacturing, for example, will need to acquire more technical skills. Today, at least one in four workers across all Organization for Economic Cooperation and Development (OECD) countries is already reporting a mismatch with regards to the skills demanded by their current job. Despite the growing need for adult re-skilling and job training, such opportunities are not currently available or accessible for most people. Millions of people transitioned out of work by machines and algorithms would deal a giant blow to global and local economies—and if left alone, the fissures from that giant crack will only continue to elongate and widen.

I view this as a once-in-a-generation opportunity to address the inevitable economic dislocation that will result from technological innovation. This means ensuring an adequate form of job security for those people who find that their careers are disrupted or replaced. It's likely that more jobs will be created than lost in the coming decade, so investing in training and re-skilling is a critical step in enabling displaced workers to reenter the workforce.

We need to do nothing short of reimagining the social contract for the twenty-first century, and a challenge this big and complex cannot be left to politicians alone. Rather than sitting on the sidelines as automation accelerates, every business has a vested interest in finding ways to train and re-skill workers for the jobs of tomorrow.

In the United States alone there are nearly half a million open technology jobs, but our universities produced only sixty-three thousand computer science graduates last year. Meanwhile, our companies can be incredible universities for educating the workforce of the future. Which is why we invest in training employees, as well as interns and apprentices, to acquire new skills, in many cases through specialized instruction and hands-on experience that can't be obtained at even the most prestigious universities.

We aren't the only ones investing in workforce development programs. JPMorgan Chase is spending hundreds of millions of dollars funding community college and other nontraditional career development programs for women, veterans, and underrepresented minorities globally. "We must remove the stigma of a community college and career education, look for opportunities to upskill or reskill workers, and give those who have been left behind the chance to compete for well-paying careers today and tomorrow," says JPMorgan Chase CEO Jamie Dimon. Dow, IBM, and Siemens have established apprenticeship programs to help fill the skills gap in their industries. And CareerWise Colorado is working to create twenty thousand apprenticeships in the state for high-demand occupations across multiple business sectors over the next decade.

At Salesforce we also use our online learning platform, Trailhead, to help both our employees and our customers continuously develop the new skills required in today's rapidly changing digital economy. With Vetforce, we offer free training to U.S. service members, veterans, and spouses to acquire the skills necessary to obtain tech jobs. I was personally inspired by TJ McElroy, who, after losing his sight in the Marine Corps, became a certified information-technology administrator through the Vetforce program. Today he instructs other disabled vets to prepare them for careers in technology.

Keith Block, our co-CEO, has taken on workforce development

as his cause, much as I have with homelessness and oceans. When he worked to launch a massive digital transformation at State Farm, he and its CEO Michael Tipsord partnered to go beyond just getting the best implementation of our software. They wanted to ensure that the workers impacted by AI-powered technology advances, everyone from the agents to the claims processors, would get the training needed to continue thriving in their careers. Part of this re-skilling is being done through Trailhead.

Keith is also committed to spreading the message about workforce development far and wide. "Get in the game," he told the one thousand partners, including IT consulting giants Accenture, PwC, and IBM, who assembled at one of our recent annual partner meetings. "This isn't only about projects or revenue; it's about truly making customers successful, and their employees."

Our companies are a vast army of millions of people who could have a tremendous impact on re-skilling workers impacted by automation: mentoring them, working side by side with them, giving them the tools they need to continue to learn and grow. By coming together not just with other companies, but also with community colleges, universities, veterans' groups, NGOs, K-12 schools, and governments, we can help close the skills gap, nurture prospective employees, and develop the future workforce that will support a strong and growing economy. It's no longer enough to bring along the workforce of *today*. We also need to work hard to build the workforce of *tomorrow*.

I often ask my peers in Silicon Valley what would have happened if the top-tier venture capital firms required the companies they invested in to put one percent of their equity into a public charity serving the communities in which they do business. The answer is obvious: Apple, Cisco, Microsoft, Oracle, and numerous other successful Silicon Valley companies would have created some of the largest public charities in the world, amassing billions of dollars that could fund programs to address the most difficult problems we face.

We need to find a way to give back on a massively large scale.

The answer is business. Some companies, such as Google, have adopted a variation of our 1-1-1 model, and we've worked with other organizations to spread it around the world. We also provided the seed for Pledge1percent.org, which encourages and provides a framework for companies of all sizes and stages to donate 1 percent of their employee time, product, and profit or equity to any charity.

More than eighty-five hundred companies in a hundred countries so far—including Yelp, TripAdvisor, Glassdoor, and Twilio—have joined Pledge 1%, generating over $1 billion in philanthropy through the 1-1-1 model. The companies understand that giving back versus looking forward isn't an either-or option. It's complementary to our investments in innovation, and the foundation of everything we stand for, because it means putting our faith in the promise of a better future.

"This is about Americans getting off the sidelines and getting onto the playing field."

These words of General Powell (who is today on the Salesforce board) have always stuck with me. Yet I'm also acutely aware that this playing field he spoke of is far from an even one, as access to education, information, and opportunity becomes more and more stratified across socioeconomic divides. And these fissures begin to widen long before people enter the workforce. To heal them, we need to start where they do—in our nation's most underserved and underfunded schools. If I could put anything on a billboard it would be ADOPT A PUBLIC SCHOOL. Or at least, donate some time and resources to one.

I believe that everyone in businesses—from the CEO on down to the summer interns—needs to begin thinking about giving back as synonymous with looking forward: as an opportunity to bring youth from around the globe back onto a more even playing field. These children are our future. Let's invest in them.

NINE

BEGINNER'S MIND

From a Blank Page to the Same Page

One of the quirks of the human condition is that all of us, at some point in our lives, will surrender to the universal temptation to kick a problem down the road. Instead of making a daily, incremental effort to address it, we'll delude ourselves—for the umpteenth time—into believing that it might resolve itself.

In June 2018, I'd reached the inevitable end of that sequence. The problem had wheeled around and started kicking *me*.

In my case, the issue was pretty simple. I was profoundly overloaded. The schedule I'd been keeping over the previous few years had drained my batteries and swallowed up most of the time and energy I should have devoted to friends and family, to relaxing and exercising, and above all, to *thinking*. Even at work, where I habitually juggled five things at once, I'd grown far too comfortable with being chronically impatient, distracted, and overbooked.

I know what you're probably thinking: *They're called vacations, Marc. Take one.* And that's exactly what I decided to do. But here's the thing: Getting away from it all was no longer a simple matter of transporting my physical person to some intoxicating, faraway locale. The only way to take a genuine break, even from thousands of miles and multiple time zones away, was to unplug from the virtual world. *Completely.*

So I decided: This would be a true vacation. That is to say, a digital detox. And not just for a day or two or even a long weekend. This time, I set my sights on two full weeks. No calls. No texts. No email. No news alerts. No Twitter.

To make the most of this rare event (and to guard against a lapse of willpower), I tacked on two thick layers of security. The first was that Lynne and I decided to visit remote islands in the South Pacific. These places are home to some of the world's most pristine, beautiful beaches and amazing biodiversity, reminders of why we'd come to love oceans so much (and devoted so much time and money to the global effort to protect them). More to the point, they were also spectacularly terrible places to get any work done.

The second failsafe was simpler to arrange, but a lot harder to swallow. On the day we left, I shut off my iPhone and iPad, stuck them in an envelope, and shipped them to our home in Hawaii, where we would return after the trip.

I didn't ghost the office entirely, of course. In the event of a genuine, code-red work emergency, I gave Joe Poch, my chief of staff, the landline numbers for the places we'd be staying. In the unlikely event that things really went sideways, I told him he could ring us on Lynne's mobile.

This wasn't the first time I'd gone cold turkey in this way, so I had a sense of how hard the adjustment was about to be. In the first few hours and days, while waiting for a flight or a seat at some seaside restaurant, my muscle memory would be triggered. I'd instinctively reach for my phone and, not finding it, engage in a few seconds of frenzied pocket patting before it would finally dawn on me. *Oh, right. I'm unarmed.*

This time, however, as I settled into my airplane seat and gazed out the tiny window at the tranquil blue expanse of the Pacific, I felt relief rather than anxiety. The last few years had blown by at a madcap pace. The list of responsibilities I'd taken on had grown so unwieldy that my gadgets had become part of my essential being. Now, suddenly, I felt liberated from them, eager to clear my head and let my mind wander.

In 1621, a Dutch physician paid a visit to the Antwerp studio of the legendary Baroque artist Peter Paul Rubens.

In addition to his paintings, which still hang in some of the world's most prestigious museums, Rubens was widely regarded as a Renaissance man. He moonlighted as a diplomat, spoke seven languages fluently, and was an accomplished art collector. He even found time to exercise. To squeeze all of this into a day, Rubens was famously adept at multitasking.

Yet even knowing this about his esteemed patient, when the physician arrived that day, he could hardly believe what he saw. The maestro stood in front of a canvas, furiously applying paint. To one side sat an assistant who was reading aloud to him from the works of the Roman historian Tacitus while Rubens simultaneously dictated a letter to another assistant. Somehow, in the middle of all that, he managed to greet the physician and engage him in an extensive conversation.

Clearly, Rubens was an exceptional person. He had a unique mental capacity to travel down several distinct paths of thought at the same time. I'm sure he would have made a formidable CEO.

The sad truth is that, try as I might, I'm no Rubens. I often wish I were, but the moments when I sense myself dividing my attention don't seem particularly productive. Research suggests I'm probably right in feeling that way. Multitasking has proven to be a pretty safe way to do many things badly.

For people who run companies, this is highly problematic. The CEO job is an endless exercise in finding new ways to squeeze work into every last corner of your waking hours. And increasingly, it's not just CEOs who feel this way. As the pace of life accelerates, employees at all rungs of a company are feeling the pressure of the never-ending workday.

But there's no question that leading a business with forty-five thousand employees and scores of customers that is constantly launching new products, acquiring companies, and investing in start-ups, all while operating a giant philanthropic arm, demands a particularly relentless pace. Although I still meditate most mornings, the moment I snap back it's off to the races. My days are packed with meetings, more meetings, product reviews, dinners, conferences, speeches, fundraisers, retreats, brainstorming sessions, media interviews, and analyst calls. It's a job that can swallow you if you're not careful.

In recent years, whether by choice or necessity (or both), the demands on my time have grown exponentially—as have my priorities. Turns out that it's incredibly difficult to scale back when *everything* seems urgent and important. However, my personal dedication to give back is non-negotiable: My wife and I have overseen nearly $500 million in personal charitable giving and serve as impact investors in for-profit companies we believe are doing positive things for the planet. And frankly, it's hard not to want to always be doing even more. I suppose that Lynne and I didn't have to decide to buy *Time* magazine in 2018, for example, but we believe it's an important institution that is having a positive global impact, and ensuring the viability of a free and open press is a cause that is deeply aligned with our values. The same could probably be said about my decision to write this book.

And while the job—and all its facets—may be exhausting, it's not a *grind*. Even those things that are born out of obligation generate excitement. I certainly don't pine for the days when CEOs clocked out at five to play golf. I love what I do.

Here's the thing: As the Fourth Industrial Revolution changes the way all of us engage with the world, such that time and space pose no barrier to instant communication, everyone involved in business has to understand that the definition of "doing your job" is subject to updating, too.

Moreover, in an era when technology is upending century-old business models almost overnight, I don't believe anyone can successfully navigate these uncharted seas without having an open mind, untethered from the past. In the future, the only way to lead a company, or even to work for one, will be to raise your eyes from the work on your desktop and take a much wider view. But you can't reimagine the world unless you learn to shield your mind from the everyday noise and chaos. Today, it's not enough to simply unplug and spend time thinking. We need to make time to think *deeply*.

At times like these, cultivating a beginner's mind and being open to new ways of thinking isn't just good for the soul, it's a survival tactic.

In a broad sense, approaching life with a beginner's mind is a way of opening yourself to curiosity, gratitude and learning. It means pulling out a blank sheet of paper. It means letting go of the idea of being an expert. As Shunryū Suzuki, a leading Zen Buddhist, said: "In the beginner's mind there are many possibilities, in the expert's mind there are few."

An expert wants to *know* things with certainty and, in the end, to be proven right. When I approach my work and life as a beginner, I'm free to let go of the past—my attachments, fears, preconceptions, even aspirations—to open my mind and heart, be in the present moment.

If my Buddhist monk friends had visited me prior to my family vacation in 2018, they would have scolded me for my habitual multitasking, for the crowdedness of my mind, and for not being fully present in any moment. As I plodded along, my window into the world we all inhabit, the world I'd committed myself to trying to improve, had gotten increasingly fogged over. This condition is not optimal for decision making. To be effective, a leader needs to both learn from the past and project the future. But you can't do either of those things until you carve out some time for being in the present.

My journey in meditation got more serious on a deserted beach in Hawaii during my lengthy sabbatical. My daily meditation and ocean swims there, often near families of dolphins, as well as my experiences in India and Nepal, allowed me to slow down and re-evaluate my priorities. I wasn't yet well versed in the notion of beginner's mind, but I knew I needed to get rid of the mental clutter that was keeping me from being fully present and open to change.

I'd always been curious about Eastern philosophy and spirituality, but as I immersed myself in its teachings and met many spiritual guides, it now took hold of me with a force that almost knocked me off my feet. I felt clear-headed, liberated, renewed. I became a firm believer in the power of meditation and the importance of practicing a beginner's mind.

I'm hardly the first business executive who's gone on a quest or spiritual exploration and come back from such a journey as an evangelist of mindfulness. From the outside, this might seem like a frivolous self-indulgence, or some flash-in-the-pan Silicon Valley fad. But I can tell you with utmost certainty, this practice hasn't just made me a happier, more productive human being. It has also been an essential *business* strategy.

If you charted all the periods of growth at Salesforce that have resulted from some major course correction I decided to pursue, you would find that those moments were nearly always preceded by a period of time when I made a point to unplug and reconnect with my beginner's mind.

After all, in times of high stress or crisis, when there's little time for careful reflection, instinct has to take over. In some ways, those decisions are the true measure of all leaders: what we do when we have to act in the moment. If you haven't taken the time to reconnect with who you are and what you really believe, those instincts will eventually fail you when it matters most.

In 2018, reconnecting with myself, my family, and with nature inspired me to act on a problem that had gone unaddressed for far too long. After two weeks of serene beaches, long walks, and life-affirming experiences in the ocean I love—the highlight was swimming with my family amid humpback whales in Tonga—I finally was relaxed and lucid enough to find a solution to my snowballing overload. For some time, my expert know-it-all mind had been telling me I had no choice but to continue operating like an octopus, casting my tentacles in a million different directions and trying to put my imprint on everything in my orbit.

Only when I was able to clear my mind did I clearly see that the numbers were not in my favor. By 2018, 86 percent of the Fortune 500 were Salesforce customers, as were nearly a hundred fifty thousand additional businesses of all types and sizes. But I was still just one person, and my obligations were growing in lockstep with our business. The more we grew, the more product rollouts, marketing campaign launches, executive development sessions, speeches, and customer meetings mandated my presence—and yet I was constantly wishing I could do more. And as overbooked, overworked, and overextended as I was now, I suddenly realized, if I kept kicking this problem down the road as I had been, it was only going to get worse.

For months, the solution had been lurking in the back of my mind, but out in those remote islands, blissfully free of distraction, it managed to work its way to the front. It was time to ask our board of directors to make Keith Block, then Salesforce's chief operating officer, a co-CEO. Keith had already taken on some of the responsibilities for running the company. But clearly, this wasn't enough. If I was to maintain my sanity and be the kind of leader Salesforce deserved, I would need Keith to step up and lead the company with me. This move, I knew, would not only take our collaboration to another level, it would accelerate our future growth.

I would continue to focus on vision and innovation in our technology, marketing, stakeholder engagement, and culture, while Keith would be responsible for growth strategy, execution, and operations.

By making Keith a co-CEO, reporting to the board and no longer to me, I would be giving up some control. But during those unplugged weeks my consciousness shifted and I saw that I needed to put more trust in the people around me. Continuing to carry the full weight of the company on my shoulders wasn't helping anybody. The new arrangement would allow me to be more mindful, more present, and perhaps less chronically late for meetings. It was a dramatic move, but one that I believe will help Salesforce prosper for many years, while also allowing me to reclaim the attention and focus that my jam-packed schedule had been costing me.

Learning to meditate is one of the best investments I've made in life. I learned much of what I know about meditation from Thich Nhat Hanh, known in many circles as the father of mindfulness, who was nominated for the Nobel Peace Prize by Dr. Martin Luther King, Jr., for his work in seeking an end to the Vietnam War. Thay (the Vietnamese term for "teacher"), as he is called by his followers, defines mindfulness as simply being aware of what is happening inside and around you in the present moment. He teaches that one doesn't have to spend years on a mountaintop to benefit from meditation. In fact, coming back to the present moment can be as simple as becoming aware of your breath. Being mindful and "present" in the moment, he says, can give everyday activities a joyful, miraculous luster. Anxiety disappears and a sense of timelessness takes hold, allowing qualities such as kindness, empathy, and compassion to emerge. It is, in short, the source of a beginner's mind.

Several years ago, when Thay was staying with me at my San

Francisco home, we meditated every morning at six o'clock. Of course, I cherished those moments with the world's greatest teacher on mindfulness, but the real lesson he imparted to me during that time came during a dinner I hosted one evening for several tech CEOs.

"Each one of us has to ask: What do I really want?" Thay said. "Do I really want to be number one? Or do I want to be happy? If you want success, you may sacrifice your happiness for it." He then explained that he had spent the day visiting Salesforce, Google, and Facebook, and described how he had seen much "suffering." People, he observed, "can be victims of their success, but no one has been a victim of happiness."

I've never been entirely convinced that the competitive nature of business today—and even the way we measure our success in it—are necessarily conducive to building a sustainably great company. But I'm increasingly becoming more convinced that they aren't conducive to achieving happiness. "What is the use of having more money if you suffer more?" Thay said. "You should understand that if you have a good aspiration, you become happier because helping society to change gives life a meaning."

I certainly don't expect everyone who comes to work for Salesforce to adopt these teachings, or to commit themselves to the study of meditation and mindfulness. As you read in Chapter 7, we have gone to great lengths to incorporate mindfulness into our culture by integrating meditation into our wellness programs and installing mindfulness zones on every floor of our office buildings. Salesforce isn't alone in bringing mindfulness into the workplace; other companies, including Target, Ford, Nike, Apple, and Goldman Sachs, also have seen that mindfulness training is good for their employees and, by extension, good for business. They understand that having a beginner's mind helps them to uncover new opportunities as well as detect signs of unrest that could cripple a company's culture.

There are many ways to practice mindfulness, of course. You don't have to take up residence in a Buddhist monastery or spend an hour each morning in meditation—although you definitely need to shut off the phone sometimes. Personally I make sure to take small moments of my day to connect with my breathing and take a step back from whatever I'm supposed to be doing. Sometimes when I sit down in a meeting, my colleagues will note that I pause for a couple of minutes and just sit there, with eyes closed and mind open. At this point my team knows me well enough to know that I'm not zoning out or sleeping. To the contrary, these are the moments that help me be fully present, and when my best ideas surface.

And yet, the most important aspect of mindfulness isn't just opening your mind or being present in the moment. It's also a matter of *listening* deeply. Not just to yourself, but to others. It sounds like a simple practice, but it's not an easy one at first, given how our minds tend to jump to conclusions, tune out what we don't want to hear, and be influenced by our moods and biases.

At a recent executive offsite, we'd concluded a difficult day of reviewing numbers and setting agendas to improve our performance. Some executives admitted to me afterward that all the tough questioning had taken a toll. I couldn't blame them; that night, even I couldn't fall asleep with all these thoughts rattling around in my head.

But the next morning, with the clarity of a rested mind, I realized that I hadn't listened deeply enough to my team. I had been so focused on the numbers that I hadn't addressed the need to relieve the tension, reduce the noise, and get back to our beginner's mind. I hadn't been listening with my heart.

First thing that next morning, I strode into the offsite and announced, "I'm going to do mindfulness with you for ten minutes." My team of forty quickly shoved their coffee, eggs, and turkey bacon aside and got comfortable.

"A lot happened in this room yesterday," I said. "We can take all of that into our heart, and then let it go and breathe . . ."

"Let's all forgive ourselves for any mistakes that we've made along this journey and forgive others," I added. "In the spirit of yesterday's presentation, may we all have the ability to speak our truth and say what we really feel and believe. And if someone needs to speak their truth to you, you're able to deeply listen. You're able to hear it in your heart."

Then I asked my colleagues to slowly bring their minds back into the present moment and the reality we faced—a thicket of numbers and nettlesome operational details.

Now, it's not often that I turn management meetings into mindfulness seminars. I'm aware that not everyone is comfortable with meditation, and I respect that view. But I can say this: At that particular meeting, the energy in the room meaningfully shifted. We all began to *listen deeply*.

The Power of an Open Mind and a Blank Sheet of Paper

I may have given you the impression that cultivating a beginner's mind and practicing mindfulness are mainly a way of summoning seismic, breakthrough ideas. That's true, but being in the present moment, paying attention to where you are and what's going on, can help us deal with those smaller, less monumental issues that dominate the bulk of our time. Whether it's a brilliant product vision that will revolutionize an industry, an idea for reorganizing your team, or tweaking a plan for growing your customer base, the devil, as they say, is in the details.

This is the flip side of beginner's mind—turning your ideas into a reality. To make it a reality, you have to convince others to align with your vision and plot a course forward. You need to *prioritize*.

And at a big company, you need to scale the process of setting priorities in order to get tens or hundreds of thousands of employees on the same page.

How exactly to do this was a problem that I'd been grappling with since the 1990s. When I returned to my job at Oracle after my first life-altering sabbatical, I was committed to growing, both personally and professionally, but the company didn't have any executive training or professional development programs. So I decided to do what millions of Americans do: I started attending seminars and taking instruction from video and yes, even audiotapes. My mentors were people whom I'd never met, like Deepak Chopra, whom I found hugely inspiring and who forced me to think about what's truly important to me, and my values. I must have listened to hundreds of hours of self-improvement lectures on cassettes in my car in those days.

During this period I stumbled into a strange melting pot of ideas. Over time, the concept of cultivating a devotion to beginner's mind and various other personal development philosophies started mashing together. It turned out to be a fortuitous combination.

At Oracle, I had just been promoted to run direct marketing and was struggling to determine what, exactly, I wanted to do in this new position—let alone what was expected of me. I had a budget, and a mandate to spend far less than I was taking in. But how I got there was almost irrelevant. There was no long-term or short-term plan. I needed a framework that was more suited to how I wanted to lead and be measured. So I began tinkering with one that would provide what I had been missing: a clear and simple way to identify our objectives, map out how we would move toward them, and, no less important, assess how well we had achieved them.

So I cleared my mind, pulled out a blank sheet of paper, and formulated a few simple questions. What is the vision for what I want to achieve? That's the first question that must be asked, because if you aren't crystal clear on where you want to go, good luck trying to get there.

The next question followed logically: What's important to me about this goal? What are the values supporting the vision?

After making a list of values, I proceeded to rank them in order of importance. It turned into a kind of binary exercise that forced me to choose between pairs of competing priorities. As I quickly learned, if everything is a priority, nothing is. I asked myself: What's more important? Is it a short time to market, or hiring more people? Is it innovation, or hitting the numbers?

It wasn't easy, but in the end I finally had clarity about how to prioritize the investment of time and money.

Once I'd identified the vision and values, I needed to establish the methods for implementing them. So the third part of the framework outlined all the actions and the steps that everyone would need to take in order to get the job done. These methods were also ranked in order of priority, and each one included an estimate of how much it would cost us.

The fourth part identified the obstacles we might have to overcome to achieve the vision. What challenges, problems, and issues were standing between us and achieving success? Which obstacles are the most critical to resolve, and how are we going to go about resolving them?

Finally, I tackled the problem of coming up with the appropriate measures: How will we know when we are successful? In my mind, a subjective yes-or-no judgment wouldn't cut it. We needed data and metrics to determine what success would look like.

This framework resulted in a process I called V2MOM, which stands for Vision, Values, Methods, Obstacles, and Measures. The V2MOM boils down to these five questions, which create a framework for alignment and leadership:

1. Vision—what do you want?
2. Values—what's important to you?

3. Methods—how do you get it?

4. Obstacles—what is preventing you from being successful?

5. Measures—how do you know you have it?

The five parts of the V2MOM gave us a detailed map of where we were going as well as a compass to direct us there. It became a major part of the Salesforce story, and a big factor in our success. Each and every time, the V2MOM process would start with a blank slate—we don't want the past to dictate our future.

Starting with a beginner's mind we could declutter our minds, dispose of outdated assumptions, eliminate distractions, and allow ourselves to focus on the what, why, and how of whatever we set out to do. Moreover, memorializing it on paper would make it far easier to get everyone in alignment. We needed to all be in the same boat, rowing in the same direction, and looking out for the same rocks and shoals that could sink our boat to have any chance of arriving safely in port with our cargo.

I also came up with four key principles for laying out this document, in addition to starting with a blank slate each time. First, everything had to be ranked in order of priority. Second, every word mattered. Third, the plan had to be easily remembered, and fourth, it had to be easily understood.

Three years later, after I left Oracle and was gearing up to start Salesforce, you can probably guess what was one of the first things I did. Together with my co-founders, I pulled out the largest sheet of paper at hand—an American Express envelope—and, on the back, scrawled out the new company's vision and values. This was the start of what became our first V2MOM, essentially our first business plan.

That first V2MOM was the start of a long journey, and looking back I can laugh at our hubris and occasional cluelessness, but we managed to achieve what we laid out on that American Express envelope.

The V2MOM became the perfect framework for engaging our

beginner's mind approach to business planning. Articulating our vision kept us grounded in reality, while writing down our values kept us in touch with our guiding principles. Naming our obstacles forced us to honestly confront what was holding us back, and quantifying what success looked like kept us honest—to ourselves and to one another.

The V2MOM would prove to be our most important management tool, guiding every decision at Salesforce and setting one uniform course for the entire company as we went from four hundred people to the forty thousand we have today. At its core, the V2MOM is a powerful exercise in alignment, allowing teams and companies to create a shared understanding of top-level priorities while providing employees with clarity and visibility into how their work contributes to the company's overall success. In my view, the V2MOM is also something more.

The beauty of the V2MOM is in its simplicity, and the fact that it works for every phase in the life cycle of an organization. We've found that the exact same structure that helped us outline our business plan as a scrappy start-up is just as effective for outlining our annual goals as a public company. I've also found that whenever we've run into an intractable problem, it's because we didn't write it down and get our mind around it within the V2MOM process.

Today, at Salesforce, we've expanded the scope of the V2MOM to both individuals and teams across the company: Each year, every single department and every single employee drafts their own. As a result, this practical exercise in raising our corporate consciousness courses through the entire organization from top to bottom. There are forty thousand V2MOMs—one written by every single employee, cascading up and down the entire organization!

And to foster transparency, we publish every V2MOM on our corporate social network Chatter instead of hiding them in a vault. And this open-book approach helps break down departmental divisions and harness the collective energy of the entire company. Anyone can look up any employee's V2MOM to see how each plans to contribute to our company's future. We even built an app that allows every employee to track their progress on each item in their V2MOM.

Suffice it to say, we take the V2MOM pretty seriously. Starting in August, I begin drafting the top-level document for the coming fiscal year with Jim Cavalieri, who was the sixth person we hired at Salesforce. Then for several months we pore over every single word with my executive team before we present it to the larger senior management group at our annual fiscal-year kickoff event in February. That's when we open up each section for feedback; we want to know how we can make the document even better. This can create some family tension as we debate priorities, action items, and other elements, but it always results in more awareness and alignment across every group.

I've also found that this process can help navigate a relationship. After the board agreed to make Keith co-CEO, we crafted a V2MOM to flesh out our new roles. Working together to identify our vision and values as a team helped us see how our skill sets could complement each other. It probably won't surprise you to learn that apart from the business of running Salesforce, we made trust with each other our top value.

I'm not sure how many of our employees have made the connection between the V2MOM process and the notion of mindfulness. But over the years, it's become clear to me that the true power in this exercise is maintaining a beginner's mind throughout the process.

But here's the thing about the V2MOM: Unlike the Lean Methodology, the Agile Method, or any number of other management trends that have caught fire in Silicon Valley, the V2MOM isn't designed first and foremost for tech companies. In fact, there is nothing tech-specific about it at all. It's a way to operationalize the vision and values of any kind of company or project.

Our chief strategy officer, Alex Dayon, for example, creates V2MOMs with customers across a variety of industries—sometimes even before they sign up to buy Salesforce technology. For example, Alex once worked with Lars Ulrich, founder and drummer of the band Metallica, to craft a V2MOM focused on helping the band to take social media engagement to the next level, further develop the brand based on its music, and be the "most socially connected band in the world."

And then there was the time he helped Stella McCartney come up with her own plan when she bought back her label from French luxury group Kering. During that critical period after regaining full control of her label, the V2MOM helped this forward-thinking designer focus on her vision for people to "look good, feel good and do good" and to make decisions driven by the value she places not only on her business P&L but also on environmental P&L. Watch for sustainable clothes from Stella McCartney one day!

Of all the things that make our culture what it is, few things get to the heart of the matter faster than the V2MOM. In fact, whenever a young entrepreneur asks me for advice, the first thing I do is pull out a blank piece of paper.

Last year, for example, I shared a plane ride with Bastian Lehmann, the CEO of Postmates, an on-demand delivery service that promised to deliver practically anything in under an hour. As an investor, I'd been sharing advice with Bastian for a few years. His start-up had created a sensation, and I found him to be extremely smart and driven.

On this plane trip, however, I could sense he was a little out of sorts. "I think you've lost a little bit of that loving feeling," I told him.

Bastian acknowledged he was feeling "a little down" over a looming restructuring and other changes in his business.

I asked him the basic questions: "What do you really want?" and "Where do you want to be?" As he began to elaborate with drawn-out answers, I cut him off. The antidote to his doldrums was obvious: He needed to get clear on the vision and values for his rapidly growing business. So, as you might expect, I got out a blank piece of paper.

By the time we landed in San Francisco, Bastian had identified the top four values for Postmates. And that night, he told me, he went home and filled out his Methods, Obstacles, and Measures. Getting back to those basics helped Postmates weather those changes that had worried Bastian, and the company has since strengthened its position as the industry leader in on-demand delivery and filed to launch an IPO.

Whatever happened to that first V2MOM my co-founders and I crafted in those early days of Salesforce? Something told my co-founder Parker Harris to hang on to that American Express envelope. He framed it and gave it to me on the day of our IPO, June 23, 2004.

Whether you're starting a business, working to create alignment within your team or organization, or tackling a personal challenge or goal, one principle holds true: Start with a beginner's mind and a blank sheet of paper.

TEN

STAKEHOLDERS
We Are All Connected on This Planet

While I was vacationing in remote Pacific islands with my family in the summer of 2018, fully unplugged for the longest stretch in years, one of the most unimaginable things that could have gone wrong in my absence, did.

All of a sudden, without warning, Salesforce became enmeshed in a heated, complex, and potentially damaging crisis. And the fact that I was off the grid would only make the fire burn hotter.

We had just set foot on the sand in Easter Island when my wife's phone lit up with the SOS from San Francisco. While I'd been halfway around the globe, untethered from—and blissfully ignorant of—what was going on at home (and for that matter, anywhere in the world), I learned that the Trump administration's immigration policy, which had already exploded into an intense and deeply emotional national debate, was impacting Salesforce in a way that I'd never considered.

These tensions had been escalating for some time, as the administration announced policy after policy that seemed designed to wrap a hermetic seal around our borders and keep immigrants out of the country. I was very vocal in expressing concerns to the administration, as was the company, about the appalling human tragedy unfolding at the U.S.-Mexico border. When reports had emerged that federal agents had been separating migrant children from their families at U.S. detainment facilities, millions of Americans were rightly up in arms. When *The New York Times* broke the story in April 2018 that more than seven hundred children, including more than a hundred children under the age of four, had been taken from their parents, it was like a bucket of lighter fluid poured on an already raging fire.

Now my team back home was sending up a flare to let me know about the existence of an open letter, written to me by four Salesforce employees and signed by 867 others, protesting what they saw as an egregious violation of the company's four founding values.

They'd discovered that the U.S. Department of Customs and Border Protection was one of our customers.

In March of that year, we had issued a press release noting that CBP had selected Salesforce to help them modernize some of its business processes. By providing the agency with access to our enterprise software, the authors of the letter believed, we were aiding and abetting the Trump administration's immigration policy at the border. They felt that doing business with CBP ran afoul of everything the company stood for, and if we allowed this to continue, it would negate the fundamental reason they'd chosen to come and work at Salesforce in the first place.

Specifically, the letter asked me to "re-examine" our contract with CBP, "given the inhumane separation of children from their parents currently taking place at the border."

"Many of us choose to work at Salesforce because of Salesforce's reputation as a company that stands up against injustice," the authors wrote. "We want our work at Salesforce to have a positive impact on our friends and neighbors, not to make us complicit in the inhumane treatment of vulnerable people." Then came the kicker: "We believe that our core value of Equality is at stake."

What they didn't know, however, was that CBP's use of our software was for very specific purposes that had nothing to do with separating migrant children from their parents—like revamping its human resources capabilities and automating some of its business tasks. But that distinction hadn't been made clear, and was easily swept aside in a heated political moment.

Because I'd been on a digital detox and slow to learn about the conflict, let alone respond, some employees had grown understandably antsy and decided to share the letter with the media. That's why I returned from my month-long and (almost) distraction-free journey of self-exploration and family time to find a small fleet of news trucks parked outside Salesforce Tower. I knew I needed to comment publicly, but before I did, I would have to listen deeply. So I set up a call with the authors of the letter.

Naturally, I've always believed in the power of technology, which is completely changing the way we interact with the world and with one another. But it's our words, not the ones and zeros of computer code, that are the most versatile and powerful tool on earth.

Most of us will use thousands of words in a typical day (I certainly do) without thinking about how quickly they can shift shape and meaning. Imagine a short sentence like "We can trust Salesforce," or maybe "We are an ethical company." Arranged in this order, those words convey a clear, precise message that, when spoken by one of our employees or customers or even someone I just met, could absolutely make my day.

Swap the order just slightly, however, and the same few words can convey something deeply disturbing.

This was one of those instances. A few minutes into the call, one of the authors had transposed two of the words in one of those sentences, turning them into a question that hit me like a gut punch.

"*Can we* trust Salesforce?"

A few minutes later, another author of the letter did the same.

"Are we an ethical company?"

In twenty years, I had never heard anybody seriously question either of those notions. Hearing this left me deeply shaken. It was one of the first times in my life that I found myself quite literally stunned into silence. It rattled me to my very core.

I've written about how a company like Salesforce cannot succeed when our stakeholders—our employees, our customers, our partners, and our communities—can't succeed. But I was quickly learning, a company *absolutely* cannot thrive and prosper at the highest levels when you lose the trust of any of your stakeholders.

The Most Important Stakeholder, for Any Company

In the winter of 2002, three years after founding Salesforce, I received my first invitation to the World Economic Forum. There I first met the institution's visionary leader and founder, Klaus Schwab.

Klaus is one of the most brilliant, thoughtful, and highly educated people I have ever met. He earned a master's degree in public administration from the Kennedy School of Government at Harvard and holds doctorates in both economics and engineering. In 1972 he became one of the youngest professors on the faculty of the University of Geneva. He founded the WEF in 1971, at the age of thirty-three; under his leadership, it has grown to become one of the most influential institutions in the world. Beyond all that, this German native is renowned for his skills in mountain climbing and cross-country skiing, in addition to being a wizard on the dance floor.

Now WEF's executive chairman, Klaus developed the concept that I consider to be one of the greatest intellectual contributions to the world of business (though when I met him in 2002, I'd never heard of it). He called it "stakeholder theory."

The first time we spoke, he'd been standing in a hotel lobby surrounded, as usual, by a throng of people he was graciously greeting. Perhaps because I'm tall and stood out from the crowd, he eventually made his way over to introduce himself. He looked me in the eyes and said a few words that are forever seared into my brain. "'Integration' is the number one word you need to think about for your business," he said. Then he walked off, leaving me to wonder what in the world he could have possibly meant.

Later that day, Klaus addressed a group of us who'd gathered for a WEF program called Global Leaders of Tomorrow. As young heads of companies and organizations, he urged us to expand our line of vision, certainly beyond our four walls and even beyond the communities we were serving. The world is filled with many different kinds of people whose fates are intertwined with ours in so many direct and indirect ways, and in our digital, connected world, our future is no more tied to our investors, customers, employees, and communities than to the global challenges impacting all of humanity: from the expanding divide between rich and poor to climate change to the intertwined problems of cybersecurity and privacy, and even, as I would later learn, a crisis at our nation's borders.

I began to understand that in talking about "integration," Klaus was urging me to look for the kinds of connections that rarely turn up in your company in-box. What Klaus was really saying is that the only way a company truly thrives is if it fully integrates into society and into the greater effort to build a better world.

Every time your company connects to another person, even tangentially, you bear some responsibility for that person's future well-being. In some ways, this is a burden, but it's also a golden opportunity. If that one small interaction can make a dent, large or small, in whatever need that person has, or whatever pressing issue is holding that person back, you will have created a lasting impression, which is the first step in building a trusted bond. Each of these interactions, in other words, is an investment in that relationship, and over many years, in the aggregate, those investments add up.

Looking back with the benefit of this perspective, I realize that my view of Salesforce at that time was pretty myopic. We had seventy thousand customers in 107 countries accessing our services, and we had committed ourselves to donating time, money, and products to good causes, but those were the only inputs and outputs I ever considered. I was not spending nearly enough time thinking about how Salesforce was enmeshed in the larger world. Running a company, it suddenly occurred to me, was sort of like standing behind a camera, and I needed to widen the aperture.

Our stakeholder group went far beyond just the people we interacted with directly in a business context. It included customers, employees, shareholders, and partners, yes, but it also encompassed our friends and neighbors, including communities and the local school systems that served them. And it even included the planet we all inhabit.

I've always felt deeply connected to the environment. Living in San Francisco and Hawaii, I am lucky to see the ocean on a daily basis. Visiting customers in cities around the world, I've seen the adverse impacts of climate change. But the events of recent years infused me with an even greater sense of urgency.

I witnessed a powerful reminder of the climate crisis we face during a panel I hosted at the World Economic Forum in 2019. On my panel were musicians and philanthropists Bono and will.i.am; world-renowned anthropologist Jane Goodall; former executive secretary of the UN Framework Convention on Climate Change Christiana Figueres; and Sompo Holdings CEO Kengo Sakurada.

In the audience was Greta Thunberg, a sixteen-year-old activist from Sweden who bravely spoke "truth to power" and has inspired youth strikes to bring about awareness on climate change throughout Europe. When I asked her to say a few words, little did I know she would outshine everyone in this room full of star power the moment she shyly took the microphone from me.

Climate change is an existential crisis, Greta began, that some say "we have all created, . . . But that is not true—because if everyone is guilty, then no one is to blame. And someone *is* to blame."

Then Greta, with her long braids, squared her small shoulders and continued: "Some people, some companies, some decision-makers in particular have known exactly what priceless values they have been sacrificing to continue making unimaginable amounts of money, and I think many of you here today belong to that group of people."

A stunned silence suddenly fell over the room. "The future of humankind," she concluded, "rests firmly in your hands."

After a long pause, there was applause, but it was of the nervous rather than robust variety. This teenage climate activist had thrown down the gauntlet to some of the world's most powerful business leaders and they weren't entirely sure how to react—not least because they knew deep down that she was right.

We can no longer deny the fact that the environment is a key stakeholder for every business—and for everyone who inhabits this planet, for that matter. We cannot sit by passively while climate change is causing our air to become unbreathable, our oceans to heat up and acidify, and our sea levels to rise. Extreme weather events—heat waves, droughts, hurricanes, tornadoes, and wildfires—are becoming more frequent, and more deadly, with every passing year. If we continue to dump plastic into our rivers and oceans at the current rate, the amount of plastics in the ocean will exceed the weight of the ocean's fish by 2050, setting off a catastrophic cascade of reactions across our ecosystem.

According to a 2018 report by the UN Intergovernmental Panel on Climate Change, humans have only about a decade to get global warming under control to avoid significant, harmful disruption. The report warned that global warming exceeding 1.5 degrees Celsius above pre-industrial levels would increase the risk of extreme heat, drought, flooding, and poverty for potentially billions of people.

As the legendary naturalist Sir David Attenborough put it, with a heavy heart, "The Garden of Eden is no more."

As the technologies of the Fourth Industrial Revolution burrow ever more deeply into our lives, we'll face what in theory should be a spectacularly easy choice. We can either use these advances to benefit the 1 percent, who already lay claim to the vast majority of global wealth and have contributed to the harm of the planet, or we can preserve the planet for generations to come. For example, will we use AI-powered drones and satellites to expedite overfishing, and underwater robots to mine and pillage our ocean floor? Or will we use drones and satellites to monitor our oceans and stop illegal fishing, and robots to track the salinity, temperature, and oxygen levels in our seawater?

The clock on climate change is ticking. And as governments and political leaders remain locked in what seems like an endless struggle to pass and enforce policies to reverse the damage, it is imperative that companies step up.

With increasing frequency, that's starting to happen. Nonprofits like B Team, which was co-founded by Sir Richard Branson, and the B Corporation are galvanizing business leaders to lead a shift to building a sustainable and inclusive economy that puts people and the planet first. They are helping to spread that message that companies that commit to responsible, ethical, and sustainable practices will be rewarded for it. As Unilever's former chief Paul Polman says, "It's not purpose ahead of profits. It's purpose that drives better profits." That's because companies that treat the environment as a stakeholder are more likely to attract both talent and customers, who increasingly demand more accountability from their employers as well as from the companies with which they do business.

Allbirds is a shining example of a company committed to treating the environment as a critical stakeholder. This fast-growing shoemaking start-up popularized ethical footwear, using wool that meets stringent standards of sustainable farming and animal welfare and that requires 60 percent less energy to produce than typical synthetic materials used in shoes. And Allbirds works with the nonprofit Soles4Souls to redistribute returned shoes to people in need all around the world.

Patagonia works to minimize the environmental impact of its supply chain, outfitting its service centers, offices, and retail stores with solar panels, LED fixtures, and energy-efficient equipment; it also donates 1 percent of its sales to nonprofit environmental groups. The outdoor clothing company is now limiting corporate clients for branded logowear to those who prioritize the planet.

The e-commerce site Etsy recently announced a full transition to carbon-neutral shipping. By committing to purchase carbon offsets to cover 100 percent of the emissions generated by package delivery, this online retailer set a gold standard for its entire industry. Even the global giants have gotten the message. More than two hundred fifty companies, including Coca-Cola, PepsiCo, and Unilever, have committed to making all plastic packaging either reusable, recyclable, or compostable by 2025.

At Salesforce we're going beyond just supporting organizations pursuing environmental change through our 1-1-1 program. In 2013, we committed to reaching 100 percent renewable energy, and we've since achieved net-zero greenhouse gas emissions globally and deliver a carbon-neutral "cloud" to all our customers. And I'm proud of the fact that in 2018 alone, Earthforce, our green team of more than eight thousand employee volunteers, collectively dedicated more than twenty thousand hours of volunteer time to environmental causes in their local communities.

We're not only instilling these values into our culture, we're also building them into our infrastructure—literally. Salesforce Tower in San Francisco features the largest onsite water recycling system in a commercial high-rise building in the United States, saving millions of gallons of water every year. For us, this is crucial, given the location of our headquarters in California, a region that is chronically afflicted by drought.

I've also made the environment a personal focus. In 2016, together with Douglas McCauley, an innovative marine scientist at the University of California, Santa Barbara, the state's leading ocean research center, my wife and I founded the Benioff Ocean Initiative. We developed a kind of research hospital for the oceans; anyone in the world can submit a problem involving ocean health and engage a team of biologists, engineers, economists, and social scientists to study it. And we're funding Friends of Ocean Action, a coalition of more than fifty leaders who are fast-tracking solutions to the most pressing threats facing the ecosystems that rely on these bodies of water.

I'm also encouraged by and supporting the Sustainable Ocean Alliance, led by Daniela Fernandez, which launched an "accelerator" program that partners start-ups with new technologies and business plans focused on improving the conservation and sustainability of the ocean.

For too long, companies have ignored or brushed off the environmental impact of their actions, claiming that it would be "too costly" or "logistically impossible" to build sustainability into their culture, their practices, and their business models. But these excuses no longer hold water. If you aren't serving the interests of your biggest stakeholder—the planet—then you aren't serving the interests of your other stakeholders either.

As former UN secretary general Ban Ki-moon has said, "We are the first generation that can end poverty and the last generation that can take steps to avoid the worst impact of climate change. Future generations will judge us harshly if we fail in upholding our moral and historical responsibilities."

He's right, of course. But when it comes to business, I'd add one more sentence. Unless you're selling real estate on Mars, the most important stakeholder for any company is the planet we inhabit now. That's not some pious piece of wishful thinking. Just widen the lens and look for yourself.

When Values Collide

Needless to say, this business of saving the planet is an undertaking of epic proportions. But as massive a challenge as it is, it does have one thing going for it: The environment is a rare issue on which everyone at Salesforce is in ironclad agreement. None of our stakeholders had any problem with making the commitments we did, and I'll admit, it's something of a relief to be (for once) campaigning for a cause everyone believes in. Unfortunately, not every pressing issue we face lines up so neatly.

As I vacationed with my family in June 2018, the company was continuing to grow at a record pace. We had been named one of the World's Most Innovative Companies for the eighth year in a row by *Forbes.* We had recently ranked as the number one CRM provider, for the fifth consecutive year. And our shareholders were pleased— from June 2017 to June 2018, our stock price increased 58 percent.

Then came the "open letter" about our work with Customs and Border Protection.

To put this letter in context, these weren't the only tech company employees taking such actions over the use of their products by government agencies. That spring, four thousand Google employees had written an open letter to their CEO, Sundar Pichai, to protest the company's work with a Pentagon program using artificial intelligence on the battlefield. "We believe that Google should not be in the business of war," the letter stated. Two months later, Google announced that it would not renew its military contract for 2019.

Employees at Microsoft that year published an open letter demanding that company executives cancel a $479 million contract with the U.S. military, stating that "we refuse to create technology for warfare and oppression" and calling for stricter ethical guidelines and oversight. Microsoft responded that it was committed to providing technology to the U.S. Defense Department and would "remain engaged as an active corporate citizen in addressing the important ethical and public policy issues related to AI and the military."

In June, when Amazon employees sent an open letter to CEO Jeff Bezos demanding that he stop providing the company's Rekognition face-identifying technology to law enforcement and other government agencies, he'd decided to push back. "If big tech companies are going to turn their back on the U.S. Department of Defense," he said, "this country is going to be in trouble."

The previous year, when the White House attempted to impose a moratorium on immigration from a handful of predominantly Muslim countries, I opposed it strongly, and talked at length about the crucial role immigrants play at Salesforce and how committed we were to protecting the rights of all people who come to the United States seeking a better life. When the Trump administration announced a zero-tolerance policy on immigration and the press began reporting on family separations, I was heartsick. It was unimaginable that families who were coming to America for a better life would be subjected to this treatment. As I thought about my great-grandfather Isaac Benioff, who came to the United States as a refugee, I promptly made donations to nonprofit groups helping families at the border.

In the United States, Americans come from many backgrounds and countries—we are truly a melting pot. Every year some of the world's best and brightest students attend our colleges and universities, and then we send them back to their home countries after they graduate. Instead, we should staple a green card to every diploma and keep them here. Our long-term competitive differentiation strategy for the United States is summed up in one word: immigrants. Ultimately, it's not AI, bioengineering, or any other tech-nology that will differentiate or make a country competitive. It's the people.

On June 14, after reading a story about fifteen hundred migrant children who were caught illegally crossing the border and then crammed into a former Walmart, I tweeted from the book of Mat-thew: "Jesus said unto him, Thou shalt love the Lord thy God with all thy heart, and with all thy soul, and with all thy mind. This is the first and great commandment. And the second is like unto it, Thou shalt love thy neighbour as thyself." I also wrote to White House officials to encourage them to end this horrible policy and reunite children with their families.

On June 17, I abandoned my phone and laptop and left for my planned vacation. A few days later, when the open letter was posted on Chatter, my chief of staff, Joe Poch, alerted the management team, who, in light of my explicit instructions not to bother me unless there was a true Code Red emergency, decided to take a wait-and-see approach in my absence. A few days of quiet went by. Then the letter leaked, and pandemonium set in.

Clearly, I had picked an inopportune time to go totally offline. When a company has an outspoken leader, there's an expectation in both good times and bad that people are going to hear his or her voice. Now the company I founded was in turmoil, and I was MIA. People began asking: "Why is Marc silent?"

On June 27, Joe finally made the call. "Are you watching what's going on?" he asked.

"How can I watch what's going on? I'm on Easter Island!" I said. "I'm not online. I have no clue."

"Well, we have a problem here," Joe said darkly.

After he gave me a quick rundown of the facts, I asked him what he'd like me to do.

"We really need you to tweet," he said. "Everyone wants to hear from *you*."

Needless to say, this phone call caught me by surprise. I was confident there had been some misunderstanding; after all, I knew that the services we were providing to CBP weren't being used to separate children at the border. I told Joe to pass that message idea along to the team and tell them to handle the situation while I was away.

I was under no illusion that 100 percent of Salesforce stakeholders agreed with 100 percent of my decisions about how to run the company. The open letter, though, was the first time that any group of stakeholders had so publicly objected to our business practices and questioned our adherence to our values. I never imagined we'd arrive there, but we had. We didn't have the option of ignoring this controversy, but the way forward was difficult.

On one hand, we had an obligation to support the employees who felt that doing business with CBP was a violation of our core value of equality and wanted us to cancel our contract. On the other hand, Salesforce wouldn't, and couldn't, cancel the CBP contract without cause. The agency was a customer, and we had a responsibility to them, and to our shareholders and investors. Either way, it seemed, we were bound to make some group believe we'd violated our number one value, trust. When the interests of one important set of stakeholders conflict with those of another, which should prevail?

That was when yet another group of stakeholders began to get involved: our customers. The last paragraph in the leaked employee letter had called for the company to craft a plan for examining the use of *all* our products, and the extent to which they were being used for harm. Some of our customers, especially those in the public sector, worried that with such a plan in place, it would be easy for us to cave to public pressure and cancel contracts at the first hint of controversy, even when criticisms were unfounded.

And they weren't shy about voicing these concerns. Keith and

Dave Rey, our head of public-sector business, and other sales executives were fielding calls from some customers wanting to know who would decide if their products were being used for good or for harm. What are the criteria, and who defines the parameters? Does every customer need to be perceived as totally aligned with Salesforce's values? Can we count on you that you aren't going to make a decision to pull your software and leave us in the lurch? This quickly became an entirely separate trust issue that our team needed to confront, and it also complicated the situation by roping in yet another of our core values: customer success.

Along with all the other firsts, this crisis marked the first time in Salesforce history that three of our core values appeared to be in opposition. Equality, which compelled us to stand up for the human rights as children were being separated from their families; Customer Success, which drives us as a company to help our customers grow; and Trust, the bedrock notion that Salesforce is a company that honors its values and commitments.

In the meantime, everyone was watching, and there were many conflicting opinions about what we should do. I knew that we needed to listen deeply to all of our stakeholders and be transparent in our thinking, but I was apprehensive about how this conversation might go. "Ethical and humane use" of our products wasn't a topic we'd had to grapple with up to this point in our history.

As more news organizations picked up the story, Salesforce issued a simple, factual statement that our CBP contract had nothing to do with family separation at the border, and that Salesforce values the equality of all. This was 100 percent true, but at the same time there was no question that by signing the CBP as a customer, we had made incidental connections with everyone that organization impacted. The next day, Keith issued a statement that Salesforce would donate $1 million to organizations helping separated families and would match employee donations to increase our impact.

With so many eyes on me, I eventually decided to break my

vow of vacation silence. "I'm opposed to separating children from their families at the border. It is immoral," I wrote using my wife's cellphone, and Joe posted the message to all employees on Chatter. "I have heard the Ohana's concerns and I'm very proud of all our employees for organizing actions supportive of families at the border."

That last sentence was not blowing smoke. I meant it with all my heart. I was proud that some employees cared enough to speak up, and question whether Salesforce was doing the right thing. And I knew the letter signed by a small percentage of our thirty-two thousand employees at the time couldn't be dismissed. They were doing exactly what we talk about every day, being part of a living, breathing, values-driven company. As I mentioned earlier, I set up the call with these employees as soon as I got back.

During the video call, the authors who had rearranged those words about trust and ethics to form those unsettling questions spoke in a forceful but nuanced way about the need for ethical use of our products and how alarmed they were about Salesforce technology being used by the CBP and their concern about the inhumane treatment of people at the border. At the same time, they seemed to want me to know that they trusted the company leadership and believed that we would ultimately do the right thing.

After I'd listened carefully to the four of them, I played back what I was hearing. Suddenly I realized that this conversation wasn't *only* about CBP. Sure, the CBP contract is what sparked it, but this was really a conversation about something much larger. This was about how our culture—as cultures do—needed to evolve. Specifically, we needed a way of ensuring that we stayed true to our core values, even when they were seemingly at odds. What these employees and the hundreds they represented really wanted was a new process and set of guidelines at the company that would evaluate our contracts now and in the future to determine whether our customers were using our technology to do harm.

Suddenly the situation began to feel a bit more familiar, and the clash of values a little less intractable. One of our key stakeholders, our employees, had identified a problem, just as they had with equal pay and LGBTQ rights. And the solution they would eventually help come up with was a brilliant one.

In the weeks after this video call, I spent a lot of time listening to our customers, our employees, our investors, and other stakeholders, including the nonprofits to whom we'd made donations of time, money, and products. These discussions brought me clarity about how we needed to recalibrate our process around determining ethical use of our technology in order to guard against unintended consequences.

Around the same time, a group of about fifty people participated in a protest in front of Salesforce Tower. They carried placards with my picture, chanted my name in various unflattering contexts, and railed that I was a hypocrite for giving hundreds of millions of dollars to the UCSF Benioff Children's Hospitals while simultaneously putting children in cages at the border.

I certainly didn't enjoy seeing these pictures on TV, or the pounding I took on social media. If previous fights hadn't thickened my skin, I'm not sure how I would have weathered this one. In my period of contemplation, I tried to focus on the truths I knew: that it didn't matter whether or not Salesforce was being unfairly portrayed in this case; what mattered was our responsibility to make sure our ethical use guidelines were clearly articulated going forward.

On July 26, I posted a statement to employees on Chatter announcing that our Office of Equality would have a new unit, called the Office of Ethical and Humane Use. It would work hand-in-hand with our Office of Ethics and Integrity, which focuses on corporate governance. We would appoint a Chief Ethical and Humane Use Officer whose newly created team would work with all of our stakeholders, as well as industry groups, thought leaders, and experts, to create, promote, and implement industry standards, guidelines, and living frameworks around the ethical use of technology.

Our first ever Chief Ethical and Humane Use Officer, Paula Goldman, describes her mission as developing a strategic framework for our technology that not only drives the success of our customers, but also drives positive social change and benefits humanity.

We all know that technology is not inherently good or bad. Much like our words, it's just a tool; what really matters is how you use it. And in the end, ensuring that it is used ethically is a central function for any business.

So the next time an issue arises over the use of our technology, we won't have to rely on instinct, or the political vicissitudes of the day, or be forced to play favorites among our core values. Instead, we now have staffed an office, assembled a diverse group of expert advisers, and created a process to evaluate the use of our technology.

I'm confident that in the future all constituencies will be heard as we weigh the ethical and humane use of our technology. But the larger point is that once again, we got through a crisis and came out stronger. And in this case, what threatened to strangle us became what saved us. It's our values, of course.

Despite all the internal angst, media hoopla, protests, and dialogue, I couldn't be more grateful to our stakeholders for sounding the alarm.

The CBP crisis was a painful reminder that even when you may think you're doing a fantastic job of listening to all your stakeholders, an existential crisis can pop up in an instant. The lesson is pretty simple: *You can't bank trust.* You can't simply fill up the jar with so many marbles that you can afford to spill a few once in a while.

Every day, every incident, every complex situation holds the possibility of a fatal misstep that tips the whole jar right over. At the same time, however, it's also an opportunity to prove how committed you are to your values—and to doing right by *all* your stakeholders.

The trick is to make sure the camera you're peering through is set to "landscape" mode so it takes in the fullest possible picture.

ELEVEN

THE ACTIVIST CEO

Taking a Stand Is Not Optional

The first rule of building a smart, sustainable business is learning how to root out complacency. Most of us in leadership roles today train ourselves to obsess over distant, scattered clouds even when the sun is bright and skies are clear. We hold strategy meetings. We indulge in worst-case scenarios. We swear on a stack of class-A stock certificates that we'll never go outside without an umbrella.

And yet, inevitably, we do.

One of the most perplexing things I've noticed about business is that there are always issues lurking on the periphery that have the potential to someday harm the company, but still, nobody in the C-suite brings them to the foreground.

There's usually nothing particularly subtle about these problems. They're often things employees discuss freely, even as most executives willfully ignore them lest we find ourselves drafted to lead some time-consuming task force. We turn away. We rationalize. We soothe ourselves by proclaiming that these issues are beyond our control and outside our defined areas of responsibility.

I'm not just talking about problems within the company, but in the communities surrounding it—problems like our struggling public schools and crumbling infrastructure.

This can happen even within companies founded with the best of intentions, as those companies grow up and become more complex organisms. The people who created them get trapped—or worse, hide out—inside the bubbles they've built, the moment the issues coming at them begin to exceed the number of hands available to fix them. All the energy that once went into innovation and scaling up can shift to another priority: the determination to protect and sustain, to simply stay afloat rather than swim.

When every crisis that pops up, large or small, starts to feel like an existential threat, preserving the status quo becomes the goal, and any deviation from it can trigger internecine warfare with a company.

In the late summer of 2018, I decided it was time for me to take on one of those issues that was on the periphery for some of my peers but had begun staring me in the face. I'm referring to the chronic, rapidly worsening homelessness crisis in San Francisco that I was encountering every day.

In a city crackling with innovation and wealth, a shocking number of people were unable to meet their most basic human needs. I've lived in San Francisco my entire life, and while homelessness has always been a part of the city, I had never seen it this bad. Some seventy-five hundred individuals and more than twelve hundred families, including eighteen hundred children who attend our public schools, are homeless in San Francisco. Many of them are living on the streets just a few blocks from Salesforce Tower. Families with children are surviving in cars, in tent encampments in city parks, and in overpacked homeless shelters. Many on the streets are suffering with mental illness and drug addiction. Heroin needles and human feces litter the sidewalks.

This crisis unfortunately isn't unique to our city—you see rampant homelessness in places like Seattle and Los Angeles. The problem is growing worse as the high cost of housing pushes more people onto the streets. In New York City, nearly 115,000 school-age children—about one in every ten students in public schools—lived in temporary housing during the past school year, a record high.

A study by the University of California, Berkeley, found that areas of San Francisco were more unsanitary than impoverished, developing countries. In 2018, a visiting United Nations official said she was "completely shocked" by the plight of the homeless in the city. And yet here we were, the masters of the new digital economy, zipping by in our Ubers and electric cars and thinking we were somehow blameless and, at the same time, powerless to act.

In 2017, a few days before Dreamforce, I walked down Third Street near the Moscone Center, where we hold the event. It was filthy, strewn with trash, feces, and drug paraphernalia. It was clear evidence that we needed to take dramatic steps to address the homeless crisis. The mayor made sure that streets surrounding Dreamforce were cleaned, but I knew then that this wasn't enough. The streets needed to be clean not just for our event, but for all residents, all the time.

The following year, when we opened the soaring Salesforce Tower, I was very aware of, and embarrassed by, the starkness of the contrast between our perch in the clouds and the streets sixty-one stories below. Inside the Tower on our Ohana floor, employees were sipping cups of espresso made fresh by baristas, taking in the breathtaking views of the city and the musical stylings of a pianist wearing a fedora playing upbeat songs. On the sidewalks below, thousands of homeless people were sorting through trash cans, some physically and mentally sick, forced to beg amongst the multi-million-dollar condos and opulent office buildings.

I wasn't blind to the fact that homelessness, and the larger economic disparities driving it, could have a significant impact on the future prospects of my company—and the entire business community in San Francisco and Silicon Valley. In San Francisco, all of the negative by-products of the digital revolution had culminated in a lack of affordable housing—and in turn, a lack of opportunity—for so many of all but a tiny sliver of the city's population. The result wasn't healthy for our fellow citizens, including some of our customers and employees, and the millions of people who visit San Francisco. And yet, for all the wealth that same digital revolution had bestowed on us, none of us in the technology industry were doing nearly enough to address the glaring by-products of the wealth we had helped create.

In San Francisco, the sad truth is that the tech industry is also largely to blame for this crisis. Our many highly paid engineers and executives have driven up real estate prices astronomically; as I write this in 2019, one-bedroom apartments rent for an average of nearly $3,700 and the median home price is a record $1.6 million. All of this has all but eliminated affordable housing, resulting in hardworking middle-class people being effectively priced out of the city.

Of course, these disparities don't start and end in San Francisco, but San Francisco does seem to be the canary in the coal mine for what's to come if we don't start addressing the harmful effects of rising inequality. On a global scale, the twenty-six richest people on the planet had the same net worth as the poorest half of the world's population, around 3.8 billion people, in 2018, according to Oxfam. About half of the people on our planet subsist on less than $5.50 a day. Even in the United States, 40 percent of adults don't have $400 available to pay for an unexpected expense. Studies by the University of California, San Francisco, have shown that children who do not have the appropriate education and healthcare opportunities by age five will remain at a disadvantage for the rest of their lives.

All of us should care about this, even if we mistakenly think it doesn't affect us directly. Because the reality is that unbridled capitalism is not good for anybody, not even all the companies reaping extraordinary riches from it. Every person on the street means one fewer person getting an education, or entering the workforce, or contributing to the local economy and community. This gulf of inequality creates the conditions that separate and polarize us, and fuel conflict.

But just because businesses like mine are a big part of the problem doesn't mean we can't also be part of the solution.

For years, I'd been partnering with charitable organizations to try to provide homeless families with some of the basic needs they lacked. I'd been working closely with mayors and other city officials to improve public education and public health in San Francisco. Salesforce became the largest private funder of the San Francisco Unified School District, and the largest single-year donor to the Oakland Unified School District. But all the while, the homeless problem seemed only to worsen.

This crisis demanded an immediate and ongoing injection of funds. We were past the point of relying on charitable donations that often slow to a trickle when another worthy or trendy cause comes along. San Francisco needed a systemic change to finance a solution for the homeless problem, and government and charities couldn't provide it. Only our city's for-profit businesses, many of which had benefited from tax breaks for locating here, could solve this dilemma.

I'd talked endlessly to fellow founders and CEOs about homelessness, asking them how they thought this was going to end up. Did they really think San Francisco could remain the world's technology capital if it couldn't provide for the basic needs of its citizens? Did they really think that the voters wouldn't get fed up and demand action? And if the people who are responsible for creating this lopsided equation won't participate in solving it, then who will?

But many of them seemed happy to remain what Anand Giridharadas, the author of *Winners Take All: The Elite Charade of Changing the World,* called the "unelected upper crust" leaving our public and institutions to rely on "scraps from winners" when we should instead take on the serious work of changing the system to change the world.

That fall in 2018, I saw my chance to do something that not only had the potential to make a real impact, but would also send a powerful message about the role of business in addressing social problems. With my visible position as a Fortune 500 CEO, I believed it was my responsibility not only to tackle this issue with every tool I could muster, but to do it publicly. It's imperative to show all our employees, customers, and peers that activism is not just the purview of patron saints, philanthropists, or nonprofits. Everyone in the workplace today has both the responsibility and the *ability* to improve the state of the world.

Before my co-founders and I hired a single employee at Salesforce, we decided that a commitment to giving back would have to be a central tenet of our culture. In the years since, I've seen how powerfully the ripple effects of this decision have reverberated across the company. But now it was time to up the ante. Taking up the mantle in the fight against homelessness, I knew, would set the tone for a renewed and reinvigorated commitment to our core value of equality.

In November, the city would vote on a sweeping homeless initiative called "Proposition C: Our City, Our Home" that would increase the corporate tax on only the largest companies in San Francisco, like Salesforce, to help finance more permanent solutions to the problem. Specifically, Prop C, as it became known, would apply a 0.5 percent tax to Salesforce and the rest of the city's biggest businesses—those that earn more than $50 million in annual revenue—to generate $300 million a year in new funds to pay for housing and services for the homeless. Individuals and small-to-medium-sized businesses would pay no tax.

To me, this plan was a no-brainer. As San Francisco's largest employer, we needed to stake out a clear position. Were we for the homeless or just for ourselves?

I decided to put my energy into getting Prop C passed. I knew that if I genuinely believed that business could be the most powerful platform for change *now*, not just in the future, this was a moment to prove it. I knew that as a company committed to equality for all, we had to support Prop C, and our executive team and employees agreed.

My efforts to get votes for Prop C started small. I began posting occasionally on Twitter. But as the importance of this opportunity and this moment became more clear to me, Prop C became my priority.

I spoke at get-out-the-vote rallies in Chinatown and addressed hundreds of San Franciscans in Dolores Park with Nancy Pelosi, our local U.S. congresswoman (soon reelected as Speaker of the U.S. House of Representatives). I hosted breakfasts and dinners with activists and advocates and became a talking head on both local and national TV news. I reviewed polling data, carried placards, tweeted campaign slogans and wore political buttons.

By the time the midterm elections approached, with the fate of Prop C hanging in the balance, I became completely locked in a fevered public battle. In my view, Prop C was a necessity for the homeless and every person in San Francisco, and also for Salesforce.

Fighting for a cause that matters to our stakeholders is just as much a CEO's job as preparing for a quarterly analyst call. Protecting the health of our community is just as much a business priority as delivering innovative technology to our customers.

Yes, I was prepared for the onslaught of criticism I knew I'd receive. But my armor had thickened. Never mind that nearly every tech CEO and billionaire in the city was lined up against me; I never felt the slightest hesitation—in large part because I'd already learned (the hard way) in those earlier fights for social justice that our employees, customers, investors, and partners didn't just support my wading into this issue. They were more than happy to shove me right into the thick of it.

But mostly, it was because all our fates are intermingled. What's good for the homeless is what's good for my company, my community, and my city.

A New Era of Corporate Social Activism

In the fall of 2015, I was invited to speak at the invitation-only technology conference put on every year by *The Wall Street Journal*. The press release touting the event described it as a summit of global technology leaders, policy makers, and entrepreneurs coming together to "focus on the global promises and challenges of today's digital world."

My appearance would involve an onstage interview conducted by one of the *Wall Street Journal*'s editors or reporters. I asked Gina Sheibley, who handled my PR, who would interview me. The answer: Monica Langley. "Never heard of her," I replied, and asked Gina to get her swapped for one of the senior tech reporters. But Gina assured me she'd done her homework on Monica. She was one of the paper's top writers, who reported on CEOs, billionaires, and presidential candidates for page-one profiles. Reluctantly, I conceded.

On the morning of the conference, Monica and I met briefly, so we wouldn't be total strangers onstage.

"Hey Marc," she said. "I want our interview to be fun!" I was fine with that, but her next sentence stopped me cold.

"I'm going to focus first on what you just did in Indiana, fighting for LGBTQ rights," she said. "And, by the way," she added, "I will introduce you as an activist CEO."

My initial reaction was confusion: Wait, I thought to myself, wasn't this an exclusive *technology* conference? I was pretty sure the two hundred people in the audience had come to hear me talk about the cloud, or AI, or my vision for a digital future. Giving an onstage interview—at a tech conference no less—about our fight to overturn discriminatory laws struck me as un-CEO-like, and downright political.

Additionally, I wasn't happy with the term "activist CEO"— not one bit. The first reason is that it sounded very different depending on whose lips it came from, and coming from most people in my circles, unfortunately, it wouldn't be regarded as much of a compliment.

The second reason stemmed from the visceral negative reaction to the idea that what I was doing was so outside the norm, or so breaking from the CEO mold, that it required a special label. Obviously, I'd never subscribed to the notion that once you become a CEO and put on that power suit, you are required to leave certain dimensions of your personality, values, and basic humanity at the door. I, for one, had refused to do so, and I knew that the company was better for it.

If you've looked at the front of this book, you've noticed that my co-author is none other than the Monica Langley who dubbed me "activist CEO."

So you can assume correctly if we're writing this book together that I proceeded to go onstage with her, despite my protestations. And you can assume that yes, she asked me about our fight for LGBTQ rights in Indiana—and in Georgia, and North Carolina. A few months later, Monica wrote a page-one story for *The Wall Street Journal* detailing how "activist CEO" Marc Benioff had "kicked off a new era of corporate social activism."

But over the next year, the term grew on me. Or more accurately, I grew into it. In 2017, I asked Monica to join Salesforce as an executive. She had seen through my defensive tactics to the CEO I was actually becoming.

Over time, I've become convinced that there are two types of CEOs: those who believe that improving the state of the world is part of their mission, and those who don't feel they have any responsibility other than delivering results for their shareholders.

In the past, I'd say that far more chief executives fell in the latter category. Their only engagement with the political process was almost wholly self-interested; it started and ended with hiring lobbyists or funding political-action committees to influence the trajectory of policy on issues such as taxes or global trade. They clung to their fiduciary duty to shareholders as their employees, communities, and the world at large took a back seat.

I don't condone that instinct, but I understand it completely. Back when I was in business school in the 1980s, I studied the immortal words of the economist Milton Friedman: "There is one and only one social responsibility of business," he wrote in his book *Capitalism and Freedom*. The answer, of course, was to "increase its profits."

In an essay for *The New York Times* in 1970, Friedman went so far as to argue that executives who claim that companies have "responsibilities for providing employment, eliminating discrimination, avoiding pollution and whatever else may be the catchwords" of the day are guilty of "undermining the basis of a free society."

With all due respect, Milton Friedman was wrong. He was wrong then and he's doubly wrong in the context of today. The business of business isn't just about creating profits for shareholders. We're simply too big, too global, and too immersed in people's daily lives. Yes, our business is to increase profits, but our business is also to improve the state of the world and drive *stakeholder*—not just shareholder—value. And not just because serving the interest of all stakeholders is good for the soul; it's because it's good for business.

The statistics bear this out. In a corporate social responsibility survey of online shoppers across sixty countries, conducted by Nielsen, 66 percent said they were willing to pay extra for products and services from companies committed to driving positive social and environmental impact. The 2018 Deloitte Millennial Survey found that millennials believe business success should be measured by more than profits, citing the creation of innovative ideas, products, and services; positive impact on the environment and society;

job creation, career development, and improving people's lives; and promotion of inclusion and diversity in the workplace as the top priorities. According to the 2019 Edelman Trust Barometer, 75 percent of consumers say they won't buy from unethical companies, and 86 percent say they're more loyal to ethical companies.

In *Fortune*'s CEO Initiative 2019 survey of eleven hundred executives, managers, and employees, 87 percent agreed that the need for moral leadership in business is greater than ever. Yet only 7 percent of employees surveyed said their leaders often or always exhibited the behaviors of moral leadership. The disconnect between beliefs and action is still enormous, and there will be consequences for business whose leadership doesn't live by values like trust and equality. In this age of instantaneous digital feedback, companies and their leaders simply can no longer turn a blind eye to the issues that matter to their employees, their customers, and the communities in which they do business.

It's not a coincidence that in recent years more CEOs are starting to speak out on social and political issues—as a matter of survival if nothing else. And let's face it, with government and other powerful institutions getting increasingly bogged down in political partisanship, brinkmanship, and perpetual gridlock, corporate participation is becoming more necessary. The deepening crisis of trust I discussed in Chapter Three, as well as the growing educational class divide, income inequality, and massive environmental challenges we face, make it impossible to abdicate responsibility and stay on the sidelines.

As BlackRock's Larry Fink has written, "stakeholders are pushing companies to wade into sensitive social and political issues—especially as they see governments failing to do so effectively," and "as divisions continue to deepen, companies must demonstrate their commitment to the countries, regions, and communities where they operate, particularly on issues central to the world's future prosperity."

That's why our businesses hold the potential to be the greatest platforms for change. Consider just this one fact: 70 percent of the top one hundred revenue-generating entities in the world are not nations but corporations. I'm talking about Walmart, Apple, Samsung, and Exxon. The people who work at these kinds of companies, from the CEO on down to the newest employee, have not only a responsibility, but also the resources, the economic muscle, and the implicit permission, to be courageous on social issues and effect real change.

I witnessed this firsthand in 2017, following the Trump administration's decision to ban citizens and refugees from seven Muslim-majority countries from entry into the United States. More than 175 companies, including Salesforce, Facebook, Microsoft, and Google, called on the U.S. Supreme Court to strike down the ban, which would inflict "substantial harm on U.S. companies, their employees, and the entire economy" and make it "far more difficult and expensive for U.S. companies to hire some of the world's best talent and impeding them from competing in the global marketplace."

Unfortunately, the Supreme Court allowed a modified version of the travel ban to stand, but by making our voices heard, we helped to shift the national conversation, drawing money and attention to the issue and creating a louder chorus of opposition as well as substantive legal challenges to government policies.

The Trump administration's withdrawal from the Paris Agreement on climate change and its decision to rescind Deferred Action for Childhood Arrivals (DACA) also motivated many CEOs and other business leaders at companies ranging from General Electric to Apple to speak out against those policies. Disney CEO Bob Iger, for example, protested the White House's Paris decision by saying in a statement: "Protecting our planet and driving economic growth are critical to our future, and they aren't mutually exclusive," and then resigning from a presidential business council.

Merck CEO Ken Frazier, GM CEO Mary Barra, and IBM CEO Ginni Rometty were among several members of President

Trump's Strategic and Policy Forum who led the dissolution of the advisory group, following the president's insistence that "many sides" were to blame for the violence in Charlottesville, Virginia, that resulted in the death of a woman when a member of a white nationalist group ran over her with his car.

There's no shortage of examples of businesses taking public stands on grave issues that tear at us as a society. After the tragic shooting of seventeen people at a school in Parkland, Florida, in February 2018, Delta Air Lines ended the discount for members of the National Rifle Association flying to the gun group's convention. When confronted with criticism from people still subscribing to the outdated idea that a company's job is purely to provide return on investment for its shareholders, CEO Ed Bastian told *Fortune* magazine, "Our decision was not made for economic gain and our values are not for sale. . . . I'm not trying to be a politician. I'm not looking to be a social activist. I'm looking to run the best airline on the planet. As part of that, we have a responsibility to our customers, employees, and community partners."

CEOs sometimes have to make decisions knowing that there could be economic consequences—that some of their customers might walk away. But no doubt just as many—if not more—would stay, because people want to do business with companies that value the same things they do.

I've long been inspired by Unilever's recently retired CEO, Paul Polman, who made activism part of his corporate strategy while at the helm. He's been outspoken in advocating for companies to produce healthier products, improve worker conditions, and adopt renewable energy sources. "We have to bring this world back to sanity and put the greater good ahead of self-interest," he has said. During his ten-year tenure as CEO, Unilever's stock more than doubled, proving again that customers are spending their money with companies who uphold the things they believe in, too.

A 2018 article in the *Harvard Business Review* perhaps summed these trends up best, declaring that "CEO activism has entered the mainstream." And according to the authors, Aaron K. Chatterji and Michael W. Toffel, this is just the opening wave of what has become the new norm.

"The more CEOs speak up on social and political issues, the more they will be expected to do so," they write, adding, "In the Twitter age, silence is more conspicuous—and more consequential."

Increasingly, companies can't afford *not* to engage on the tough issues, if for no reason other than the fact that their employees demand it. The 2019 Edelman Trust Barometer found that 71 percent of employees surveyed said it's critically important for their CEO to engage on challenging issues, and 76 percent of the general population said that they want CEOs to take the lead on addressing societal issues rather than waiting for governments to weigh in. Businesses that ignore these imperatives stand not only to alienate their clients and customers, but also the best and brightest talent.

We used to think of customers, employees, and communities—local and global and everything in between—as different constituencies. But really they aren't so different after all. They're all a part of the larger ecosystem that our companies serve. And they're united in demanding that we not only deliver them innovative products they want, but also that we deliver on our commitment to uphold the values they care about.

Our Civic Duty, and Our Corporate Responsibility

Hundreds of companies have already shown that doing well and doing good are not in opposition. That's why, by the time Prop C came along in the fall of 2018, I no longer felt that we were rolling a rock up a steep hill alone. Turned out, I wasn't completely right, though.

I'll admit, my support for the homeless was personal. At the start of the book you read about how, as a boy, I always was struck by how my grandfather, Marvin Lewis, gave $20 bills to homeless people we passed in our city walks. Grandpa also advocated for the homeless as a city supervisor. One of my favorite stories about my grandfather is about the time he attempted to show a short movie about homeless children living "just a few blocks from the city's finest shopping district" at a San Francisco Board of Supervisors meeting. The mayor blocked him from doing so, but Grandpa never gave up the fight.

So maybe I was simply channeling my grandfather when my wife, Lynne, and I began working to help end the plight of the homeless, especially homeless families in San Francisco. In 2011, we read a story by Jill Tucker in the *San Francisco Chronicle* about Rudy, a homeless fourth grader. She wrote about how Rudy, along with his younger brother and parents, would spend nights sleeping in homeless shelters, bus stop shelters, and parks. On weekdays he would take two buses to get to his elementary school, tired and hungry.

Since then, Lynne and I had given nearly $20 million to fund housing and services for the city's homeless population. In 2016, we contributed $10 million in matching funds to the city of San Francisco's Heading Home Campaign to end family homelessness, and in 2018, we gave $6 million to the Bristol Hotel Housing Project to transform a hotel in San Francisco's Tenderloin neighborhood into housing for the homeless. Salesforce.org has given nearly $6 million to help end homelessness.

For years, I had also attempted to persuade others to join us, going hat in hand to make my case to nearly every high-net-worth individual in the city. But as I was learning, philanthropy alone won't provide the systemic change to make a real difference to homelessness and other societal problems.

I didn't expect an unbridled endorsement from the tech community on Prop C, but I was still surprised that many businesses and individuals flat out refused to support the new tax. Companies including Lyft and Stripe, as well as venture capitalists like Michael

Moritz and Paul Graham, donated money to the "No on Prop C" campaign. Some individuals actually called and asked *me* to oppose it. I listened to their business-based arguments. They would say that Prop C lacked sufficient accountability and that a corporate tax addressing one problem was the start of a slippery slope. It could lead to more taxes for a range of social issues in the future. Then there were the optics: Going out on a limb to campaign *for* a tax increase—corporate suicide! But I felt the crisis of homelessness was so important to address for our city that we had to be for it.

In response, I told anyone who would listen to take a look at our fourteen-year stock chart for proof that our investors aren't complaining about Salesforce giving back to the communities where we live and work. Quite the contrary: In 2018, even as the overall market had its worst year in a decade, our shares rose 31 percent. Since becoming a public company in 2004, we delivered a 3,300 percent return to our shareholders by June 2018. Those are sure signs that doing good aligns with doing well.

Some companies opposed to Prop C claimed that their main concern wasn't for their profit margins or share price—they said they were opposing the initiative for the good of the city! According to this backwards argument, the tiny one-half of 1 percent tax on their revenue above $50 million could render rents even more unaffordable and drive their companies—along with the jobs they created and the taxes they paid—out of the city. I doubted their logic, and it made no sense to me that they couldn't see homelessness as more of an existential threat to their business and community than a relatively painless incremental tax.

I presumed that my fellow industry leaders had watched closely as Amazon had defeated a corporate tax proposition in Seattle earlier in the year. But I was determined not to let them follow that playbook. And I was grateful that a couple of business leaders, including Chuck Robbins, CEO of Cisco Systems, and venture capitalist Peter Fenton, publicly supported Prop C.

Still, Prop C was an underfunded and underdog measure on the November 6 ballot. So I rallied my troops. I presented a plan to the Salesforce executive team, whose members were quick to agree: As a company committed to living our values, Salesforce would contribute $5 million to the effort to back the campaign, and I personally donated $2 million to the cause. Employees in our government, legal, and public affairs departments also pitched in. We produced TV spots urging voters to approve the ballot measure, pointing out that individual residents wouldn't pay a penny to fund the homeless programs—the tax would hit only big corporations like ours!

A month before the election, Prop C was losing, according to the polls. I then launched a campaign of nonstop tweeting, media appearances, and speeches. It was exhausting, I'll admit, but I was hell-bent on doing everything in my power to try to turn it around.

My guiding light during the Prop C campaign was our city's namesake and patron saint, Saint Francis of Assisi, who inspired me with these words: "Where there is darkness may we bring light . . . and where there is despair, may we bring hope." And finally, "For it is in giving that we receive."

Ironically enough, it was the vocal opposition from a fellow tech CEO that ultimately began to turn the tide in favor of Prop C. With less than three weeks to go before the election on November 6, Jack Dorsey—the founder and CEO to two San Francisco tech darlings, Twitter and Square—responded to one of my many tweets supporting Prop C: "I want to help fix the homeless problem in SF and California," @jack tweeted. "I don't believe this (Prop C) is the best way to do it."

My response was immediate. "Hi Jack," I tweeted back. "Thanks for the feedback. Which homeless programs in our city are you supporting? Can you tell me what Twitter and Square & you are in for & at what financial levels? How much have you given to heading home our $37M initiative to get every homeless child off the streets?" I already knew the answer: zero.

Then I pointed out how Jack had created $50 billion in market cap with Twitter and Square, and had raked in more than $6 billion personally, all the while taking special tax breaks for locating their offices on Market Street, one of the city's main thoroughfares. "Exactly how much have his companies & [he] personally given back to our city, our homeless programs, public hospitals, & public schools?" I asked, rhetorically.

Of course, the media had a field day with our "Twitter feud," as they liked to call it, with headlines from TECH TITANS BATTLE to TECH BILLIONAIRES GO TO WAR OVER HOMELESSNESS. One might think that the coverage would have overwhelmingly supported my position, but not so. *Inc.* magazine wrote: "Not content with antagonizing Zuckerberg, Benioff has also taken on a slew of his fellow tech billionaires. . . . Like the Mothra-fighting Godzilla of later films, Benioff doesn't *need* to be doing what he's doing." And *Fast Company* magazine accused me of "Twitter-shaming" Jack for being antihomeless.

On that point, I was guilty as charged. I framed it as the binary issue I believed it to be: You're either for the homeless or you're for yourself. I sang that chorus from the rooftops—and eventually my city listened. My feud with Jack Dorsey turned Prop C into the hottest issue on the ballot, and on November 6, Prop C passed by a strong margin—61 percent support.

This new funding for the homeless, some $300 million a year, was earmarked to address the crisis from every angle. It will provide more than a thousand new shelter beds and four thousand additional housing units, and up to $75 million will be allocated for treating the severely mentally ill. In addition, the funding will provide assistance or subsidies to help thousands of residents avoid eviction, a measure critical to preventing San Franciscans from becoming homeless in the first place.

Within weeks of Prop C's passage, big tech and other local companies got the message. Many of their employees had been disappointed with their leaders' failure to do the right thing. These companies began to realize that their employees had the same kinds of expectations as customers. And that in an employment market as tight as the tech world in San Francisco, keeping these other "customers" happy was just as important. We all know that talented tech workers will have no trouble finding a new perch if they aren't happy in their current one, and that includes feeling like the company they work for doesn't share their values.

That's why in San Francisco, Airbnb is now spending $5 million on homelessness, and Twilio CEO Jeff Lawson donated $1 million to fund homeless services in the Bay Area. In Seattle, Microsoft has launched an affordable housing institute and Amazon is giving money and space on its campus to help the homeless.

Businesses, which have historically been wired for anti-tax positions, may finally be realizing that they now need to take the lead in putting our communities and countries first by supporting mechanisms that will generate funding to solve our most urgent problems.

In reflecting on the Prop C battle during the months after its passage, however, I was struck by how many people had opposed it—not just CEOs who stood to absorb the tax increase, but ordinary San Franciscans who witnessed, every single day, the suffering of their fellow citizens living on the city streets and yet voted against a measure designed to fix it. That's when I realized: It wasn't that the Prop C opponents didn't care about homelessness, it was just that they had different ideas about the best way to address it.

This insight inspired Lynne and me to fund the $30 million UCSF Benioff Homelessness and Housing Initiative, aimed at building reliable and credible science-based research to help policymakers, community leaders, and the public understand how people become homeless and identify solutions to alleviate the crisis.

The world badly needs a North Star for truth in homelessness. Data is crucial for ensuring that we invest in programs that can make a real difference in addressing homelessness and housing. For example, data shows that providing permanent supportive housing for chronically homeless adults creates long-term housing stability in over 85 percent of the people housed and often does so with an overall reduction in government expenditure. Dr. Margot Kushel, the director of the initiative, is leading the research team that studies factors such as poverty, domestic violence, age, family size, and unemployment office visits, to design the most effective ways to prevent and end homelessness.

By leaning on medical science, emerging research, and data, my hope is that we'll no longer have to argue about what works best. Instead of letting our gut instinct, assumptions, and the partial truths fed to us by snake-oil salesmen and politicians inform our position, we'll simply let the science be our guide.

Because once we stop fighting one another and start working together, change can happen. It's our civic duty *and* our corporate responsibility.

Businesses don't have all the answers, of course. And neither do the people who lead them. In fact, it's often the people sitting as far from the C-suite as you can imagine who emerge as the most impassioned voices for change. These are exactly the people we need to come along and pierce our bubble, jolt us out of our comfort zones and remind us of our responsibilities to our communities and to one another.

Hundreds of millions of people around the world get up and go to work every day, and they shouldn't have to leave their values at the door. Employees who feel empowered to express their views on the tough issues are not just better employees, but more fulfilled people. And when we as leaders speak out for the causes *we* believe in, we inspire employees to do the same. Regardless of our individual values, or the specific issues we choose to crusade for, by making *action* a cultural norm, we empower everyone in every workplace to be a trailblazer, an activist, and an agent of change.

Imagine a future in which CEOs and their companies around the world applied the same focus and innovation they bring to solving their most complex business problems to solving our most complex social ones. Together, we can make that future a reality by creating cultures of activism where every individual is personally invested in making the world a better place.

EPILOGUE

In January 2018, in the early stages of writing this book, Salesforce Tower officially opened for business in San Francisco. At sixty-one stories, it's the city's highest structure and one of the tallest skyscrapers west of the Mississippi.

I won't lie—I was thrilled. I had spent years on this project: finding the right location on Mission Street and then tinkering with design details, from the multicolored furniture in the lobby to the artistic tiles on the walls. I knew its completion marked a significant milestone in the company's history.

I couldn't have been prouder. I also knew some people would hate it.

To many outsiders, this tower emblazoned with our name could be seen as a garish, glass-paneled obstruction of the city's iconic skyline. They might view it as a monument to some rich guy's runaway ego, or a symptom of his edifice complex. That's all fair enough. I understand where the eye-rollers were coming from. Many people associate gleaming skyscrapers with the worst kind of corporate extravagance.

I also knew that in this case, none of those criticisms were true. On a basic level, I regarded this tower as an homage to my beloved grandfather, Marvin Lewis, and his passion for inclusive progress. As you might remember from earlier in the book, he was the driving force behind BART, another San Francisco construction project conceived on a grand scale. To truly serve its citizens, he believed, a city must *grow*. And no city grows without builders, or high ambitions.

I also wanted the tower to make a powerful statement of loyalty to my hometown. With this tower, we were planting Salesforce's headquarters in downtown San Francisco permanently. We were sending the message that we were here to stay. We would not be fleeing the city for the conveniences, cost efficiencies, and tax advantages we could have reaped elsewhere. Big office towers hold the promise of more jobs and support scores of new businesses. We intended to make our presence meaningful and beneficial to our community.

I understood that the new sixty-one-story skyscraper would raise our profile and subject us to heightened public scrutiny. After all, a sixty-one-story glass tower is a terrible place to hide. So in my mind, Salesforce Tower was also an expression of our commitment to transparency, and our number one value, *trust*.

In the years leading up to the opening ceremony, our values had become deeply woven into the fabric of the company. I knew they were strong enough to outlast my tenure as the company's leader, and I trusted that whoever would fill that role in the future would elevate our values even more. So why not raise a structure everyone can see?

The only bittersweet feeling I had during the ribbon cutting stemmed from the physical absence of the two people who inspired the journey that brought me to this place: my father, Russell Benioff, who died in 2012, and my grandfather Marvin Lewis, who died in 1991. I knew they were there in spirit, but I would have given anything to see the expression on their faces as they gazed up at this building. Recalling my walks through the city as a boy with Grandpa, however, I'm pretty sure he would have approved.

A few days after we moved into Salesforce Tower, I felt the urge to abandon all my unpacked boxes to take a walk outside. I had a feeling where I might end up, and two minutes later I arrived at the Embarcadero BART station, the one that many Salesforce employees pass through every morning on their way to work.

But I wasn't catching a train. I'd come to visit a little-noticed granite plaque affixed to the wall. It's dedicated to my grandpa.

Every time I walk by this station, I stop to read the inscription, which calls Marvin Lewis a "mass transit pioneer" whose "crusading spirit," and "unflagging perseverance" presented the city with a gift of "unmatched value."

I'll admit it's over the top. But remember, these words were composed in a less complicated moment in time when people were far more inclined to believe in heroes, even flawed ones. My grandfather was a wonderful man, but he certainly wasn't perfect. Nobody is.

The truth is that this bustling station started as a murky vision in one man's imagination. And there's no question that it came with its share of untold costs and complications. But two other things are also true. First is that BART has become an essential portal and economic engine of San Francisco. And second, the incalculable value it has created grew from the *values* that inspired it.

In my mind, this tower is a monument to the trailblazing spirit I aspire to live by: to the idea that in the future, the highest form of business value will be the kind guided by the highest human values.

The first time I heard Klaus Schwab use the term "Fourth Industrial Revolution," a cartoon lightbulb popped on in my head.

I'd long suspected that the rapid pace of technological change I had seen in my lifetime was unique in human history. Of course, I understood the concepts of recency and magnitude, which suggest that it's always tempting to look at what's happening around you and conclude that it must be extraordinary. But Klaus convinced all of us that it really was.

Throughout history, scores of intrepid and optimistic individuals and movements have blazed trails for later generations to follow. Over the last seventy years, we have seen dark times, but also incredible leaps of human progress: the steady erosion of global poverty, the rise of literacy with broader access to education, the spread of democracy and free market economies, and the absence of apocalyptic wars, to name a few. People born today are likely to live longer with fewer immediate threats to their well-being.

That said, we've got a lot of work to do. The rising temperatures threatening our ecosystems, the plastics polluting our oceans, and the global deforestation occurring at a rate of an acre per second certainly come to mind.

The Fourth Industrial Revolution has given technology the leading role in this unfolding story. And how that story ends will depend entirely on what we choose to do with the advances this era has wrought. On the one hand, advances in AI, quantum computing, robotics, connectivity, and genetic engineering can be applied in ways that will make us healthier, safer, and more prosperous. At the same time, if we're not careful, these innovations could be used to further exacerbate inequality, speed up the destruction of the planet, and inflict catastrophic harm.

In a way, the term "industrial revolution" is misleading. Technology might be accelerating the pace of change and upheaval, but the next revolution will be characterized by something less tangible. It's not about embracing new machines, or new technologies, or even new ideas—it's about adopting a new mindset.

In the past, we relied on advancements in technology, business, science, and medicine to improve the well-being of humankind.

But the Fourth Industrial Revolution has brought us to a new in-flection point. From here, the marginal benefits of the technology itself will begin to decline, while the complexity of its unintended consequences will grow. If we don't act now, those two forces will eventually intersect and the costs of rapid change will begin to out-weigh the benefits. Put simply, we're at a crossroads, and the actions we take from this moment forward will have a defining impact on what kind of world we leave behind for future generations.

I'm going to make a bold statement: Future historians may not agree with me, and you certainly don't have to, but I think it's time to consider whether the Fourth Industrial Revolution is coming to an end, and to make way for a new era.

We have lived through a period of exuberant innovation and creativity. The Fifth Industrial Revolution is about finding ways to harness all of this "progress" for the common good. In the future, success will depend on whether the fruits of that innovation and creativity are used in ways that put the well-being of our people and planet first.

In this footrace between progress and destruction, we can't waste time trying to pick winners and losers. Our fates are tied. We need to start driving a different kind of global agenda oriented around making the world a more just and equal place, while also undoing the damage we have caused to our skies, oceans, and for-ests.

In the spring of 2019, as I write this, I've been thinking about the generations that will dominate the workforce in the coming years. The 2018 Deloitte Millennial Survey found that millennials and members of Generation Z want their business leaders to be proactive in making a positive impact on the world, as well as in preparing their organizations and employees for the changes wrought by the Fourth Industrial Revolution.

If that's correct, the implications for business are staggering. Now and in the future, the character of the work people do, and the nature of their workplace environment, will mean more than the superficial trappings of "success" businesses have focused on in the past.

This is not about shiny modern office towers, of course. This Deloitte study, together with many others, has shown that today's workers, especially younger ones, are increasingly devoted to serving a higher purpose at work. And businesses that fail to satisfy this basic human need will find that their days are numbered.

For businesses that want to thrive in this coming era, the question is no longer: *Are we doing well?*

The question is: *Are we doing good?*

In these pages, I've tried to show you how these questions have become inextricably linked. As the Fourth Industrial Revolution continues to reshape our lives, it's no longer an option to do well without doing good. In the face of the inevitable disruption ahead, we need to get to a place of what I call *radical* trust, where employees and other stakeholders *no longer need to demand* that companies apply their values for good. Empowered by radical trust, every business can nurture a values-based culture and become a powerful platform for change.

The actions we take from here will determine how this story ends, and I don't expect them to be easy. But I have many reasons to be optimistic.

I'm optimistic that we can build companies, governments, and organizations that are trusted, dedicated to the success of all stakeholders, and drive innovation that changes the world for the better. I'm inspired by the idealism and actions of thousands of young people I've met, not just in business but in every setting. They're not sitting on the sidelines. They're speaking up at work and supporting their beliefs by volunteering time, donating money, engaging on social issues, participating in rallies and protests, and making decisions, as consumers that reduce their impact on the environment and reward companies that do the same.

I'm also convinced that we can make workplaces more inclusive, and by doing so, make better business decisions. Only once everyone—of all genders, races, ethnicities, and orientations—is represented at the table will we be able to fully tap the invaluable wisdom people have gleaned from their own different backgrounds and experiences.

I decided to call this book *Trailblazer* because at its core, this book is about leading the kind of change that will define the successful companies and individuals of the future. Usually, however, when business leaders talk about the change and innovation of the future, they are looking at a horizon of five years or three years or one year (if not next quarter). But being a true trailblazer requires we take a longer view; by that I mean twenty, fifty, or a hundred years—maybe even longer. If this seems extreme, just imagine yourself sitting in a rocking chair in the twilight of life wondering whether you should have done more to help save the planet or end homelessness or ensure equal education to all. Imagine what you might tell your grandchildren, or your great-grandchildren, if *they* asked you whether you should have done more.

Being a trailblazer isn't just about caring for today's stakeholders—it's about creating a better world for future generations of stakeholders as well.

I humbly, and urgently, invite you to join me.

ACKNOWLEDGMENTS

In this book, I've written about our four core values at Salesforce, and how values create value. Embedded in every one of those values is gratitude. After all, we are all connected, and none of us can accomplish anything meaningful alone. It's important to stay humble and value the contributions of all the people who have inspired you and lifted you up. And gratitude is an essential part of trust, because by acknowledging our appreciation for those who have trusted us, we are paying that trust forward.

Without the support, encouragement, and trust of our stakeholders, Salesforce would be just another company. That's why every presentation any Salesforce executive does around the world—whether it's my keynote or a customer presentation or an internal meeting—starts with two words: *Thank you.*

We are thankful because we recognize that everyone has a choice. Our customers can choose one of our competitors. Employees can choose to work somewhere else. Partners can choose not to support our products. Shareholders can choose to invest in other companies. Our communities can choose to reject us. We are grateful for the opportunity to earn their loyalty rather than have it handed to us.

With gratitude in mind and the book at a close, I thank first and foremost the employees, customers, and partners of Salesforce, who inspire me every day. I want to thank all those in our communities who also inspire me every day to be a better person.

Usually a business leader sits down and writes the book in a cocoon, as if he or she has all the answers. Well, as you know by now, that's not me—and that's not Salesforce. After all, this book isn't just about my journey as a CEO. It's about our journey as a company, and as an Ohana, our extended family of stakeholders.

One of the things I talk about in the book is how, in a world where everything and everyone is connected like never before, you can't wall yourself off. That's why I shared drafts with my colleagues at Salesforce—hundreds of them—as well as friends and advisers. Their feedback was invaluable.

I don't know if a CEO has ever written a book this way—but that's what I mean by looking for innovation everywhere, from anywhere.

I'm grateful to my co-author, Monica Langley. Without her amazing effort, this book would not have been possible. In addition to being a Salesforce executive vice president, Monica managed every aspect of the *Trailblazer* journey. We spent endless hours together eliciting stories from my childhood to the present that would illuminate how I came to believe that business can be the greatest platform for change.

I also thank Dan Farber, a Salesforce communications executive with deep knowledge of the company and the tech world, whose writing, editing, and counsel were essential to the book. Sam Walker, author of *The Captain Class: A New Theory of Leadership* and a columnist and former colleague of Monica's at *The Wall Street Journal,* enriched these pages with his adept and insightful edits. And I'm grateful for Talia Krohn, our incredibly thoughtful and gifted editor at Random House, who immersed herself in Salesforce culture, even spending an entire week at Dreamforce!

Monica and I also want to express our gratitude to and love for our families.

Finally, with the book at a close, I am truly grateful to everyone who took the time to read my story.

INDEX

gender equality and, 102
  innovation as foundational
      principle, ix, 28, 85
  integration into society and
      building better world,
      188–89
  meditation and, 171
  redefining, 75–76

C

Camp B-Well, 135–36
Capitalism and Freedom
      (Friedman), 212
Carey, Matt, 73, 75
Cargill, 133
Carranza, Richard, 159–60
Castile, Philando, 112
Cavalieri, Jim, 181
CEOs. See executives
Chang, Emily, 109
Chatter (social collaboration
      application)
  features, 41
  grievances aired on, 45–46
Chatterji, Aaron K., 216
Chopra, Deepak, 177
Chouard, Kim, 148
Cisco Systems, 154, 219
Clinton, Hillary, 29
Coca-Cola, 192
College Track, 114–15
companies
  balance between trust and
      growth, 38–39

demand for socially responsible,
      35, 212–13, 216
  examples of socially responsible,
      210–11, 214–16
Compassionate Capitalism
      (Benioff), 8
complacency, 203–4
continuous iteration, 52
Conway, Ron, 159
Cook, Tim, 31, 33
Corbett, Bill, 135–36
corporate culture. *See also* values
  authenticity and genuineness as
      necessary, 124, 125
  defining, 129–30
  as determinant of business
      success, 21–22, 126
  examples of, 132
  importance of ability to evolve,
      126, 199
  need to continuously nurture, 131
  principles needed to guide, 129
  trust as basis of, 125
corporate culture of Salesforce.
      See also Salesforce values
  as embodying *Ohana*, 132–34,
      135–36, 137–38, 145–46
  fun and play, 141–42
  philanthropy and, 22–23,
      153–58, 192, 198, 207, 217
  psychological safety and,
      138–40
  totems, 124–35
  volunteerism and, 22, 130,
      147–50, 155, 160, 192
corporations. *See* companies

E

T

ABOUT THE TYPE

This book was set in Garamond, a typeface originally designed by the Parisian type cutter Claude Garamond (c. 1500–61). This version of Garamond was modeled on a 1592 specimen sheet from the Egenolff-Berner foundry, which was produced from types assumed to have been brought to Frankfurt by the punch cutter Jacques Sabon (c. 1520–80).

Claude Garamond's distinguished romans and italics first appeared in *Opera Ciceronis* in 1543–44. The Garamond types are clear, open, and elegant.